Aftershock

Aftershock

Reinventing Myself
One Piece at a Time

Penny Fisher

E. L. Marker
Salt Lake City

E. L. Marker, an imprint of WiDo Publishing
Salt Lake City, Utah
widopublishing.com

This book is a work of creative nonfiction. It is a product of the author's memory, which is flawed. Several names and personal details have been changed; others have not.

Cover design by Steven Novak
Book design by Marny K. Parkin

ISBN 978-1-947966-62-8

This book is dedicated to my two darling children,
Ross and Sloan,
who gave me the will to survive and thrive.
I love you both infinitely. Mama.

Introduction

This book is not for the faint of heart. My sojourn from coma to consciousness, through heaven and hell to reclaim my body and soul, is my personal version of my favorite book, *The Odyssey*, by Homer.

"His descent was like nightfall" —Homer, *The Iliad*

Lord, help me! I was so sick, to the point of madness, years ago in a California emergency room, dying of toxic and septic shock, knowing full well I was losing the fight but unable to speak up and change the course of my demise.

Have you ever had dreams where you try to save yourself from harm, but you can't because your are frozen and unable to stop the imminent tragedy from happening? If only my experience had been a dream. Had I been able to express my thoughts that night, devastated and full of fear on a hospital gurney, I might have been able to save myself from what soon became a real-life nightmare.

I knew I was dying that night. My internal organs were shutting down and my screams for help were only in my mind. I couldn't get the attention of the doctor, who seemed detached and disinterested, and my husband at the time, who was there physically, seemed more inconvenienced than concerned.

In that small sterile room, which smelled of hospital cleanser and the remnants of Thanksgiving, my spirit quickly drifted away, and no one stepped forward to pull me back. As the doctor and my husband both ignored and interrupted my already weak communication attempts, I heard God's voice telling me I would suffer grave consequences for staying silent in such a pivotal moment.

I felt remorse but still could not speak, even though I knew I was in imminent danger. The men in the room had spoken and I, dutiful to the end, had agreed to be silent. Little did I know how not using my voice in that moment would have dire, lifelong consequences.

From that moment forward, I no longer existed. The Penny I had been for nearly fifty years simply ceased living. Through a long, dark winter, I was on my own, fighting to survive, experiencing what felt like endless loneliness through time and space.

The seventy-five days I spent in a coma were like swimming through a black ocean at night in a starless sky, with nothing to navigate my way home. Just lost at sea, alone, disoriented, and supremely frightened. How did I physically survive? A team of prolific doctors and scientists still ponder this question with no clear answers. My recovery was hailed as a miracle by my family and by a shocked team of doctors stunned by the entire experience. As improbable as my physical survival was, my emotional recovery was even more formidable, considering the challenges, handicaps, and uncertainties I faced.

I've learned that I am hard to kill both physically and spiritually. It has been an uphill battle, overcoming relentless physical pain and chronic sickness while learning to cope with artificial limbs and disappearing fingers and raising two children through a tumultuous divorce.

But despite it all I finally reclaimed my life in ways that are better than before. I now make decisions for myself that feel right and organic.

This book is meant to raise awareness about advocating for oneself in times of fear, sickness, and extreme duress. By sharing my story, I hope to inspire women who are unhappy, to let them know they have the power to make a change.

Sometimes we *do* get to choose whether we live or die. Fortunately, I had the chance to make that choice. I chose life!

Prologue:
My New and Surreal World

R oss, I can't find my finger!"
 I am frantic, smack in the middle of Bloomingdale's in New York City, searching the floor for one of
my fingers.

I am in the middle of a weekend getaway to bond
with my nine-year-old son and show him what I love
about this bustling city I once lived in while working in
the fashion industry. After some sightseeing, sauntering
down Madison Avenue, and after a great lunch, we are
doing a little shopping.

"My finger fell off!"

"Where is it?" Without hesitation or panic, Ross
springs into action and helps me look. We get on our
hands and knees, blurring the real and surreal as we try
to locate one of my five prosthetic fingers. As horrifying
as this might sound, it is not an uncommon occurrence
or even the most humiliating.

I glance at my first-born son, a child who emanates so
much comfort and joy. Something about his smile and

quick wit always puts me at ease, but maybe not today.

"Mom, don't worry. We'll find it."

This is another moment when my reality begins to spin. It's a crisp, picture-perfect October day. I'm wearing my brown shearling coat and riding boots, feeling like any other Midwestern gal from Chicago on a visit to the Big Apple. I am happy and present, loving this moment as a mom and a living, breathing human being who has survived a near-death experience mostly intact.

But as I crawl around on the floor, hoping no other limbs fall off my body, the idyllic, warm picture I had of myself and my son becomes smeared in a muddle of black and grey.

How many times had I searched the floor of my house for an earring or a car key, giving it little to no thought? Probably more times than I can count. But a finger—my finger—in front of so many people in the middle of Manhattan's most famous store? That was a first.

How is my son handling this? What about my daughter and my husband back home, still coming to terms with a wife and mother dancing through life after they thought she never would?

"Excuse me, ma'am," a security guard says. "Can I help you?"

Ross stares at me, probably wondering how I will respond. Am I accepting this new truth, the fact that one of my prosthetic fingers has popped off during my son's long-awaited weekend get away with his mom?

If a director suddenly yelled, "Cut! Scene!" I would not be surprised, because I feel as if I am on a movie set, acting out someone else's life. Just one year ago, my world was full of friends and fashion, glamour and excitement, young children, a cherished family, travel and exercise, joy and laughter. Then, in the blink of an eye, what used to be "normal" became my past. My days now consist of doctor visits, treatments, rehab, fear, loss, and pain. But I refuse to let any of that define my world. With a loving family, devoted friends, and some brilliant doctors, I continue to re-paint my landscape and fill in my new form with changing colors.

Right now, those colors are the tiles on the floor of Bloomingdale's and all I can hear is my breathing and the sounds of more security guards approaching.

Who I have become does not resemble who I used to be. Yet, I am here, almost fifty, and it's still me. I'm even laughing about it from time to time as I try to sail through these days with a smile on my face and gratitude in my heart.

"I found it!" Ross says, holding up my finger for everyone to see.

I go to grab it quickly, but then slow down, loving how my smart, industrious, amazing son is so cool and helpful as I ease my way forward. He's putting his Humpty Dumpty mother back together again.

I grab Ross' hand and together we walk out of the store and into the sunlight, heads held high.

Chapter One:
Youth

"Life is largely a matter of expectation." —Homer

In the years preceding my life-threatening illness, I had my share of triumphs and challenges like everyone else. Some were unexpected, including the tragic death of my grandfather when I was a little girl, a booming business gone bankrupt, a brief but doomed marriage, a seemingly charmed second marriage which produced two lovely babies, and the unfair loss of my mother to cancer right before the birth of my first child.

All these experiences served as a backdrop to the most unexpected and sudden challenge of all—surviving death along with the collateral damage it brought in its wake.

As a little girl in the upscale suburb of Skokie, just outside Chicago, I enjoyed a privileged life, full of toys and fancy dresses. I remember sitting with my grandfather at a restaurant called Fritzel's somewhere under the train tracks in Chicago. Fritzel's was my favorite place to eat when I was very young. It represented the glamour of the old city, and it was usually a prelude to a visit to an art museum or a fun walk along the "mag mile," or Michigan Avenue.

When I went out with my grandparents, my father's parents, I always wore my Saks Fifth Avenue best, including kid leather gloves and a wide brimmed hat. I felt fancy and grown up. My grandfather couldn't look at me without chuckling; although only five or six, I wanted him to take me seriously. My grandparent's environment was one of taste and elegance. It was a lifestyle I loved, and it became my standard for how I wanted to live my life.

They were native Chicagoans who lived downtown in a chic, Art Deco apartment with views of Lake Michigan and Buckingham fountain. They filled their beautiful home with artifacts collected on their many trips all over the world. I loved spending time with them and learned about art and culture at a diminutive age. Their lifestyle made perfect sense to me. They enjoyed good food and lively, meaningful conversations. My childhood in the suburbs barely resembled that urban life I loved.

My mother's side of the family was also wonderful and unique. They lived in flower- filled homes in the sunny suburbs of Los Angeles, where I spent many vacations. This experience also left an indelible mark on me. The beauty of California was magical, and I loved the fashion and home design of that time and place in the late 1970s.

Seeing these two sides of life, I felt excited and hopeful about my future. The world looked exciting to me, and I was motivated to work hard and make a great life for myself, one full of interesting people, travel, fashion, and success.

I also learned at a young age that many good dreams can come to an abrupt end, like the flip of a switch things can go from light to dark.

When I was ten years old, sitting on a school bus about to go on a field trip, someone called my name and pulled me off the bus. My grandfather had died in an electrical fire in the furniture store he owned with my father, Donald, who survived.

This event marked the end of my blissful youth. My grandfather, the patriarch of our family, had provided us with affluence and safety. Our family was devastated and quickly spiraled into financial hardship. Unmoored without his father's strength and support, my father never fully recovered emotionally or financially from this loss.

After my grandfather's store burned, my parents kept me on a tight leash. There were no more regular visits to the city. I became a passionate reader to fill the hours; I was nearsighted and awkward. I loved the comfort and entertainment of having a book under my nose for most of my free time.

High school was better than my turbulent middle school years—more relaxed, with new friends and more independence. I don't know how I passed high school, since I never studied or did any homework. Later, I found out I had ADD, but in those days, the learning challenges it presented were never addressed by schools, doctors, or parents.

Life at home was chaotic. Like many of our friends' parents at the time, ours often left my brother and me alone. Whenever our Aunt Myrna came to visit, she tried to provide some structure and direction, but that was fleeting and didn't offer any lasting cohesion.

Then I became attractive to boys! I wasn't unique in that respect, because boys at that age flipped out seeing any girl become a young woman. One day, a kid stuck his hands down my shirt in front of everyone, including my teacher, who ignored it. The buttons fell off and my bra was torn. When my mother called the principal, he blamed me for dressing too provocatively. Despite that, my looks became what made me feel good, and I loved developing my own unique clothing style. I identified myself by how I presented myself to the world. For me, high school was all about having a good social life.

After years of feeling indistinguishable from everyone else, my looks helped me stand out. I wasn't the only beauty in school or amazing in any way, but my appearance became the one thing I could count on to get me noticed and make me popular.

That was my talent, or so I thought. I worked hard to present myself a certain way each day and relied on my appearance for acceptance. Through the years, especially when I left home to venture out on my own, I depended on being pretty.

Chapter Two:
Fashion

"The journey is its own reward." —Homer

I enjoyed and understood fashion, so I pursued it as a career early on with zeal and earnestness. I left college and embarked on a global career in fashion. I saved enough money to move from my parents' home to Chicago and got a nice apartment downtown. I relished the city life, especially in my early twenties. By the time my peers came home from college, I was already up and running in my own successful design and sales firm inside the Apparel Mart of Chicago. I was successful and independent. I was living as I had always imagined I would— free and traveling and meeting new people.

The Apparel Mart of Chicago was the Midwestern hub for offices that sold clothing to the brick-and-mortar stores of the Midwest. After almost a year of pleading for a sales job within one of my favorite showrooms in the mart, I got hired and quickly became the top salesperson. The company was named Condor, and I loved working with the clients, building sales departments dedicated to our great fitting slacks with coordinating tops. My boss was an endearing if unpredictable man named Ross, and we had a great working relationship.

I loved my job and made great money at a very young age. I moved into a beautiful apartment near the lake and made many new friends. I went out every night and was still with my college boyfriend. I felt happy and invigorated.

Suddenly without warning, everyone I worked with was fired from the main corporation and they brought in new management. I was the only one left standing. The meanest and nastiest woman and her miserable Doberman of a brother came in and instilled fear and dread into my heart. I knew my days were numbered; they were using me until they knew the ropes.

My boyfriend and I broke up. I wanted to date others, and he accepted an out-of-state job. I got severely sick with mono and had to move back to Evanston with my parents because I couldn't work. I cried every day for months and gained thirty pounds from inactivity. Being back home was not where I wanted to be. I needed my great life back, so I returned to the Mart and found another job where I met a talented designer. She gave me my start as an independent sales rep for her clothing, and from there I began to build a company selling multiple lines of women's high-end clothing. I went on the road driving from town to town in my beautiful clothes, driving through middle America and stopping at truck stops, staying at flea-bag motels. I wanted so much more than that. I began to work on my next move.

I enjoyed being self-employed and had fun at work, but the physical work was grueling, especially traveling alone for extended periods of time. But it allowed me to afford to move back into the city, where I could begin again and enjoy nights out dating and seeing friends.

A big part of my time was spent at the health club across the street. The East Bank Club of Chicago in its early days was the premier health club, a happy and fun place. I met many interesting people who are still great friends. Often after work I went to an exercise class or for a swim. Invariably I would meet someone new and usually agree to a spontaneous dinner date.

After many scary winters of driving through white-outs, I decided to take my business to a bigger level by designing a small collection of my own. I designed skirts and flattering, body-contouring jackets in unique fabrics, pieces to elevate a young career wardrobe. I would pair these waist-cinching jackets with one of the skirts or a fitted dress or a pair of tights and some fabulous boots.

I made my production manager my equal partner and our business took off instantly. The first collection shipped and sold out in one weekend. We had people waiting to order more, some big businesses backing us, and we grew quickly.

Our company, Desert Nights, should have endured; but sadly, it takes more than a great product and high sales to ensure business stability. So many aspects and challenges were thrown at me, and I was able to overcome all but the final one that put us out of business.

—⁓—

My girlfriends and I were young, upwardly mobile, fearless femme fatales. We enjoyed a constant revolving door of illuminating first dates, but we all secretly wanted to meet our future husbands. I had many dating adventures, and my friends and I constantly shared funny stories about our dates. *Sex and the City* had nothing on us.

Although I dated a lot of interesting and affluent men, I was most attracted to edgier, long-haired, free-spirit types. They were a rarity in my circle, though. Many of the men I met were charming and interesting, and it was fun getting to hear their stories. I wasn't always looking for love—instead I looked for entertainment and good companionship, if possible.

One day as I was getting dressed in the locker room at the East Bank Club of Chicago, a random woman approached me. She wanted to introduce me to her friend—she thought her friend and I would be a good match. The interaction wasn't too strange—after all, the locker room at the "EBC" was a social event within a social event. Without too much questioning, I dutifully followed her out of the dressing room, more from sheer curiosity than interest. Curiosity and fun have always been high priorities of mine. My need for both tended to land me in precarious situations resulting in funny stories to entertain my family and friends.

I followed the lady from the locker room into the bar to see a handsome and distinguished older man with astonishing blue eyes staring at me intensely. Before I could say hello, he loudly exclaimed, "How blooming young is this girl? I have a daughter probably not much younger than her! She's much too young for me, for goodness' sake!"

I giggled at his blustery attitude, and we began to quip with one another. I was late for another date, but this older gentleman named Paul intrigued me. I loved his confidence, humor, elegance, and class. Paul was devilishly handsome with an aura of danger and mischief. I had yet to meet anyone so dynamic and sophisticated.

However, he was right to let me marinate.

Years later, my roommate Heather and I met for dinner one evening. As we waited in vain for a table at the packed café, I was surprised to see Paul approaching us. He gallantly invited us to join him and his friend. I felt concerned because Heather knew how to bewitch men and, even despite our age difference, I still liked Paul enough to worry about him swooning over my gorgeous blond roommate.

After dinner when the time came to leave, Paul offered to walk me to my car. Outside, he whispered in my ear, "You are amazing, Penny, but you are still too young for me."

I turned to look directly at him and said calmly but coolly, "It seems to me, Mr. Eddie, that I have the upper hand here in the age category so it should be my choice." With that, I jumped in my car and drove away irritated and dismissive. As I sped away, the look on his face said, "Touché."

Some years later, as I walked alone by the lakefront after a rainstorm, a solitary figure appeared through the mist. It was a happily surprised Paul who said, "Penny, I've been looking for you lately. I'm ready." Typical of Paul, whose personality and lifestyle were unusually dramatic.

He had a stone mansion that took up an entire city block on the most illustrious street in Chicago. The courtyard housed multiple homes for his extended family. Although Paul's estate was less than two blocks away from my apartment, it was more than a universe away from my cozy abode.

Most evenings I dressed in my finest self-designed clothes and walked down the street in my stiletto boots to his mansion. With dark mahogany and velvet décor along with Paul's handsome formality and intensity, everything about him and his house gave off vampire vibes. I couldn't help teasing him about it, which he good naturedly admitted to having heard previously. I had no idea how old he really was, but he seemed to never age.

Our time together was like a fantastic dream, simple and gorgeous. Paul had a flexible schedule, allowing us to spend a lot of time together. He was generous and smart. After a delicious meal or after a party, we would stay up late talking about weighty issues. I greatly admired his intellect. Although arrogant and intimidating, he had integrity and principle. He was honest, often brutally so, but also loving and supportive. I could live with his brashness, which I found entertaining. Paul had admired my style and creativity as an upwardly mobile fashion designer creating my own brand. He was proud of my accomplishments and my then-thriving business.

With Paul, I lived a charmed existence where common problems and daily grinds ceased to exist. A butler stood outside our bedroom door taking breakfast orders for a world-renowned chef to prepare a gourmet breakfast for us. Classical music played at all hours. Freshly cut floral arrangements in ornate crystal vases appeared weekly throughout his home that was as extravagant as a small palace.

Our conversations were lively, and our time together was peppered by visits from his family and friends, prominent figures in the Chicago area. We were in love, and I was in awe of this life with Paul. When we discussed marriage, the subject of children was our biggest obstacle. Paul was already a father to adult children with grandchildren forthcoming. His kids were like my own peers and friends.

While I respected his position, I could not commit to giving up on motherhood with children of my own.

I wanted it all. Marrying Paul would mean days spent in pursuit of my own personal pleasure. Despite an exciting life filled with operas, premieres, and beautiful environments, how can a woman give up the opportunity of motherhood, if that's what she always saw in her future?

Paul understood my dilemma; he had amazing kids and he wanted no less for me. I rolled the dice and chose to explore my destiny as I moved forward down a very different and challenging path. One looks back to those forks in the road and wonders at what might have been, but my decision allowed me to become a more aware and evolved person. The love and sanctity of motherhood opened my heart in ways I never could have imagined.

I stayed good friends with Paul. Sometime after our breakup he sent me an invitation for a formal party at his compound. Heather intercepted and opened my personal mail, somehow knowing which letter contained his invitation. I still have no idea how she knew to open that one. Normally, she brought in our mail and left mine on the counter.

Heather was determined to go to this party whether invited or not. Paul confirmed that she was *not* invited; he considered her a calculated schemer who took shameless advantage of me. Of all my friends, he cared for her the least.

Heather insisted on attending anyway, and she came solo with her head held high. Her boldness paid off in spades, because there in Paul's magnificent lair she met a high profile, but married, celebrity.

As I sipped champagne in the moonlight, she ran up to me breathlessly. "My favorite newscaster is here!"

She spent the rest of the evening flirting with him, pulling out all her stops. And it worked. Heather, a Marilyn Monroe–type, had a profound effect on most men, and this man was no exception. Heather wanted the ultimate catch: somebody with clout, prestige, and money and she'd found all of that in him. Their love affair worked out despite heavy odds against their favor.

Heather climbed her way up the social ladder to the highest heights and afterward, she only called me to brag about her exploits among the elite. The man left his wife, and they have been together since as quite a power couple. Although Heather got her every wish, she had to agree to his one stipulation. She must forego her own personal dream of motherhood based on his desire for freedom. Much like my own crossroads, Heather had a choice, and she chose differently than I did.

I watched from afar as a barometer of what might have been had I chosen differently. Her life path was far easier, but possibly less complete. I didn't really know or care. I had some unfortunate circumstances that derailed the life I had chosen for myself. I loved being a mother but I suffered in a lonely and inept marriage and for that I railed upon myself; but my children were the product of that union and have been the touchstone in my life. My children were the reason I chose to live when I was given the choice. Being a mother opened my heart and transformed me in the best ways possible.

—⁓—

There were times through the tough years after my illness that I was barely surviving both physically and mentally, suffering through every pain and humiliation imagin-able and asking myself how I got here. Once or twice from a pain-laden stupor, I switched on the television to see Heather and her husband looking every bit the power couple, all dressed up on the news and attending some fabulous event. It looked so easy and civilized and like the life I had given up. Instead, I walked and stumbled on the infinitely harder road.

I had looked forward to great things in my life and been thrown crazy curves. Ever since, I spent my days trying to figure out the how and why of it all to no avail. I have spent time and hard-earned money on healers and spiritualists and therapists and doctors and specialists and have found no answers.

I suppose there are no obvious answers or reasons for our biggest life events. And so, not always sure how, I try to make the best of what cannot be changed and to live each day in joy and gratitude.

Chapter Three:
Betrayal

"Why so much grief for me? No man will hurl me down to death, against my fate. And fate? No one alive has escaped it, neither brave man nor coward, I tell you—it's born with us the day that we are born." —Homer

My business endeavors took me from Chicago to New York, Hong Kong, and Europe. I loved being creative. Designing and selling clothes was my passion and talent. My strength was merchandising the collections, my favorite aspect of design. I had a vision, and I knew what would sell, where it would sell, and to whom. Selling and designing clothes was my one natural talent. My career became my personal identity and a real source of pride for me.

When it all came crashing down, I was nearly destroyed. The failure of my company was not due to lack of sales or poor design, which were my personal responsibilities. Instead, our failure came from the production side when thousands of garments were manufactured in mismatched and flawed color dyes. This was my partner's major responsibility.

We had sold over 800 stores worldwide, but we could not overcome this disaster. We'd incurred too much cost from making the garments and returning them, unable to re-sell them as they were defective. A matching collection that did not match. It was crushing to have had this happen after so much hard work, creativity, and success.

Somehow my partner was able to convince our investors at the bank that I was to blame, so that she could move forward on her own with their investment group. She spun a completely untrue story and hatched an incredible plan while I was on the road with our upcoming collections. I came home after three weeks to find myself locked out of my business and all of our bank accounts.

I walked away with nothing, not even a photograph of the beautiful things I had designed and sold. She maligned me so thoroughly that our investors distanced themselves and forced me out.

The paper trail spoke for itself and proved my innocence. Months later the truth came out and her solo career folded. I barely felt any glee upon hearing this, as I had been nearly destroyed. It took a toll on me for years. I was able to quickly reinvent my career, but my business was a tragic shell of what it had once been. My promising future was trashed.

That experience rocked my self-confidence and shook me for years. I had been stoic in my self-defense, urging everyone who questioned me to look at the facts, but the damage had been done.

This was my first adult experience redirecting myself under severe duress, and I made it to the other side quickly. But it was terribly painful to be falsely accused of doing something illegal. I had founded and developed a design company using everything I had, only to be forced to walk away with nothing to show for it after knowing success and realizing our great potential.

I felt robbed of that opportunity. Our product was clever and beautiful, and I had sold it to wonderful stores for their customers. I had to reinvent and redirect myself, as I tapped my inner strength and courage and kept moving forward.

After she locked me out of the company, I gathered information to defend myself then I flew to New York and cold-called fashion houses. I even walked into their offices without an appointment, trying to create a position for myself. Within twenty-four hours, I secured a high-paying position designing a new clothing collection. I spent several months in Hong Kong, an amazing experience. The rest of the year I spent in New York, selling the collection we made in Hong Kong.

I was emotionally and physically wrecked from the break-up of the company in Chicago, but I pulled off a wonderful gig, which rejuvenated my soul. After my business partnership collapsed into bankruptcy, I discovered the resourcefulness required to survive a crisis and rebuild, a lesson I would apply many years later.

I pivoted my job from being the designer and salesperson of my own small line with becoming the head designer for a global firm with massive resources and factories in China.

I moved into this new life in Hong Kong excitedly, although still suffering from that awful experience of being falsely accused. I hopped on a coach flight to Hong Kong, not knowing how long I'd stay there or even where I'd stay. I was to meet the owner who I met only once before during our interview at Hong Kong International Airport.

Working for this company was fun, exciting, and lucrative. Experiencing and working in Hong Kong was dynamic; I met incredible friends there, and the people at work were talented and capable. It healed me from the stress and sadness I felt from unfairly losing everything I had worked so tirelessly for.

Chapter Four:
Marriage

"If you serve too many masters, you'll soon suffer."
—Homer

Once I moved back to Chicago, I was excited to reconnect mind and body with a few lovely men. But like many single women, I grew tired of answering questions about why I wasn't married at thirty-five.

When I met Jim, I wasn't taking life seriously, certainly not with him. A mutual friend warned me that although he was sweet, handsome, successful, and came from a great family, he would not be my type. In addition, I was dealing with problems at work, and after learning my mom's cancer was terminal, I had little to no capacity for taking on a serious relationship.

Maybe it was a challenge or just lowered expectations, but I enjoyed our first date. I liked Jim's eyes and his mellow, awkward demeanor. He was complimentary and sweet but a bit square and boyish compared to most of the men I had dated. Something about him seemed worth getting to know better, so I agreed to a second date.

I considered canceling that date due to the stress at home and work. My mother had no more than eighteen months to live, making it difficult to think of anything else. At work, the clothing line I had represented as my comeback in the clothing business went bankrupt, owing me $60,000 in sales commissions I had no hope of getting. I had done a spectacular job placing their product in the clothing stores around the Midwest and now had nothing to show for it.

I thought maybe my date's calm demeanor would help. I imagined him listening to me intently while holding my hand, softly cooing support and understanding. I wore my orange and pink retro wrap dress by DVF and greeted him warmly. We sat down for dinner at a restaurant called Rhapsody, located in the Orchestra Hall building near Michigan Avenue. That's when he suffered a full-blown panic attack.

As we were served our appetizer, Jim broke out in a cold sweat and told me he was having an anxiety attack and needed to get up. I helped him pay the bill with his credit card and tried to calm him down. His eyes were glazed over, and he mumbled incoherent gibberish. I took him outside to flag a taxi to take us to our respective homes. This was far from the comforting evening I had imagined. I just wanted to get home, but Jim did not want to leave his car there and he didn't want me to leave him.

We took a long walk down to the lakefront. I had to hold his arm and speak soothingly to him. I had no idea why he was in this state and I never found out. Sometime later, he said it could have been from a long day of golf.

My mother was terminal, I was broke, and I had agreed to forego any settlement from my brief first marriage, a blip on the screen of my romance resume. Now, there I was, soothing a spoiled, confused man-child.

Jim followed me home and to my girlfriend's apartment. I could not wait to get rid of him and was relieved when he finally felt capable of driving himself home.

He became even more persistent in the months that followed. Not only did I have the look he liked, buy I was also kind and empathetic to him. A moth to a flame, as they say. Jim clung to me like crazy glue, especially when he realized how caring and understanding I was. He set his sights on me, first by making me his girlfriend. He was depressing, pessimistic, anxious, inexperienced, and six years younger than me. I fought him off and tried to ditch him, but he would just not get lost.

At this time, friends wanted me to meet a newly single man named Tom. We went out in a group; I found Tom fascinating and attractive. He was close to my age and a self-made global success story. He was fun, exciting, dynamic, and irreverently funny. We had instant chemistry. For several weeks, we barely spent our free time apart. There was one slight problem, though. Tom was still reeling from a break-up with a woman he loved madly and had lived with for years. She had moved out because he didn't want to marry her and have more children. Tom had been married before and now raised his three kids with his ex. When I expressed to Tom that marriage and children were my ultimate goals, he reassured me by saying he might consider that with me. At thirty-six, I was was too afraid to take the risk and get my heart broken, so I backed away.

Years earlier, during my relationship with Paul, he had proposed marriage on the condition that I would forego having children of my own. While I was not ready then for motherhood, I didn't want to commit to never having them. I had plenty of time yet to settle down. When the time was right, it would happen. I looked and felt much younger than my age. None of my close friends had been pregnant either. We were just enjoying our lives!

Jim's tenacity wore me down. It started on that second date and carried on right into our marriage. No matter what the issue might have been or how I may have objected, when he wanted something, be it dinner or sex or a TV show, he was relentless until I finally gave in. That may have been due to my tendency to please, because when people pushed hard enough, I would politely succumb, yielding to a fear of getting hurt or even worse— hurting someone else.

Jim asked if he could just be there for me as a friend if not a boyfriend. *Sure, why not?* I gave in half-heartedly. I reasoned he would care for me and be a plus one, but in hindsight, his depressing demeanor only brought me further down. At some point, I just gave in and went with him on vacations and to meet his family, whom I loved. He tended to blurt things out that seemed out of sequence. I would nod and only half listen. My brother and my dad were quirky, too, so I was probably more accepting of his strange personality issues than most women would be.

Once Jim got me as his girlfriend, he set his sights on marriage and children. For some reason, underdogs brought out the Robin Hood in me, so I guess I took my love for the rich and gave it to the poor. It was easier being with Jim than continually trying to resist him, despite seeing plenty of red flags and my reservations about us as a couple.

My divorce from my first husband was finalized in April and my apartment lease was up at that same time. Jim prevailed on me to give up my little place and move into his Lincoln Park townhouse. I barely remember the details surrounding that move. I was not myself. I was now financially dependent on someone else for the first time in my adulthood. I had worked long and hard for those commissions and was gifted in that industry. I had left all my marital assets in my first marriage in order to move on. I'd retired from the apparel industry, which I loved and was great at. By that time, the wholesale fashion industry was based in Manhattan, and I needed to stay by my mother in Chicago. I had already lost my dad from a sudden heart attack about five years earlier. I had an older brother who lived in California. I took my real estate exam and passed. I took a job with a realty group and modeled part-time to supplement my income. With time on my hands, I became more involved with my new boyfriend and his family.

One beautiful spring day, Jim called. He wanted me to arrange an appointment with my gynecologist, as he was worried that I was too old to produce children at thirty-seven. He wanted assurance that I could conceive before he committed to marriage. I was completely caught off guard by this but agreed to set up the meeting that same evening. Doctor Toig, my gynecologist, assured me that I was healthy and able bodied.

That night, Jim took me to dinner and convinced me to go off birth control. He also once again mentioned signing a prenup. I am normally pretty feisty, but at that time I was not, being submerged in my own problems. I was unsure of my mother's future as well as my own. I lived with Jim but felt unsettled.

Three weeks later, I was pregnant. Instead of feeling happy, I was reticent. Jim barely moved from the bed as I emerged from the bathroom holding the blue stick. I don't think we embraced. He had just smoked pot, and marijuana made him even more mellow and difficult to comprehend. Shortly after, he went into the bathroom to write a marriage proposal on the mirror. He thought it was cute and I thought it was sad.

Jim Fisher was the third child from a well-known Chi-cago family. His mother was a celebrated beauty queen who had left Jim's father for their best friend when Jim was a toddler. His older brother was a knockout with his mom's glamour and sex appeal. He was also a star athlete, popular, a good student, and a complete girl magnate. Another brother was smart and savvy. Jim was quiet, lonely, and depressed. His father moved to California, let his boys run his successful business, and saw them for vacations.

Jim yearned to have what his brothers had—young children, a pretty wife, and a home in the northern sub-urbs. He wanted children to grow up with his nieces and nephews and I seemed like a good vessel.

I sleepwalked into the arrangement he wanted. Now that Jim had the girl and was on the way to having his first born, his next project was to get married and have me sign a prenuptial agreement. I tried to be understanding, but I felt it was unnecessary and overly protective. He knew I had dated men far more successful and wealthier than he, and if that were my agenda he wouldn't have been in the running. He also knew I took nothing from my prior marriage. I was no opportunist.

Since I was pregnant, Jim immediately began plan-ning our wedding. I had already been married once and had a wedding that felt wasteful and extravagant. I was pregnant and unsure of my own feelings. I did not want a big, lavish wedding. My family had no money. I confessed my doubts to my mother's sister, Myrna, who was always there for me. We were closer than mother and daughter and both gravely concerned for my mom. Aunt Myrna saw my marriage and my pregnancy as an opportunity to have a safe and good life with children of my own. I swallowed my doubts and focused on my blessings.

Jim and I had already planned a summer trip to Europe as he had never been overseas. Our ten-day trip to Italy was planned for September 6th and our wedding date for September 30th. The trip, the pregnancy, the wedding—it was all happening too fast. Jim said his lawyer was drawing up the prenup and I needed to get my own lawyer. I hired a friend of a friend named Steve Rizzo.

The morning of our flight, I became violently ill in the shower, I threw up and fell because I was overheated and lightheaded. I was miserable and crawled back to bed. I knew this was only morning sickness, but I felt horrible. My fiancé was unsympathetic. He walked ahead of me at the airport, forcing me to run with my bags that he refused to carry. I was upset and concerned, noting I was sick from being pregnant with our child. He snapped at me that I was always too slow.

Once we settled into our seats on the aircraft, I tried resting my head on his shoulder. He took his hand, cupped it on my forehead, and pushed it away from him. I was appalled and upset. The next move my future husband made was to produce a thick, multi-paged contract for my review. I said if he showed me that again, particularly on my honeymoon, then the engagement and the trip were over.

Jim reluctantly put the contract back in his briefcase but promised it would reappear once we were home. When we got back, his stepdad picked us up. We were arguing and I told him about his stepson pushing my head back, which still upset me. He said he was concerned that we should not be getting married now, only fourteen days away. I was doubtful and felt trapped.

Chapter Five:
Regrets

"The roaring seas and many a dark range of mountains lie between us." —Homer

The next morning, Steve Russo called to say the business prenup contract was far more extensive than just a protection for the business. Steve, a lawyer for marriage contracts, told me this was the most one-sided, unfair, and cruel contract he had ever read. It had me waiving all my marital rights, and he could not and would not allow me to sign it. He felt I should not marry a man who would insist I sign such a contract.

I felt physically sick and betrayed, and my mind shut down. I couldn't imagine my future husband was as bad as that. I felt trapped. I spent the days leading up to my wedding trying to figure out a plan. I could not. I spent the next thirteen days arguing with him about the contract. He insisted that all the other women in his family signed it, so I had to sign it, too.

On September 29th, my family met for our rehearsal dinner, and I introduced them to Jim's family. The only person missing was the groom! I called to see why he was not there, and he said it was because I had not signed the prenuptial agreement.

I was humiliated. I drove back home. I couldn't cope; I didn't like the person Jim was and didn't feel I should marry him, but I felt stuck, as if I had nowhere to go. I did not want to burden my dying mom and move in with her when I was three months pregnant. I had fantasies about rekindling with Tom and running off with him but knew that I could not because I was pregnant with another man's baby. I stayed up all night on the phone, trying to figure it out.

My future mother-in-law said we shouldn't get married based on how awful things were between us. Jim insisted we married as soon as I did the right thing and signed the contract. I didn't sleep that night and was very troubled the next morning. Aunt Myrna told me to call my attorney so we could go over the agreement. I was anxious and felt duped. Had I known before going off birth control that my future husband was this kind of person, I wouldn't have gotten pregnant or agreed to marry him. Now Jim had me in a horrible position.

At noon on the day of the wedding, Aunt Myrna and I arrived at Steve Russo's office. He had told the attorney to double the alimony, which was still insultingly low. Jim had made $489,000 the previous year; however, the alimony initially was only $25,000 per year for five years, allowing my $125,000 total. Steve got the amount doubled to a one-time payment of $250,000, but it was still only half what Jim made in a single year.

The contract went on to say that I was not entitled to anything unless I personally had sweat equity in procuring the money. Jim wanted me to be a stay-at-home mom without any rights because I didn't earn anything; and he wanted me to waive every single right provided to married women.

My attorney was kind and patient and asked if he could go over the contract with me paragraph by paragraph, but I could not process what he was saying. There were two hundred people showing up in four hours to see me marry someone who everyone thought was a nice, loving guy.

"You are not marrying into a family," Steve said. "You are marrying into the mob. I would not sign this, Penny. Walk away."

He would not give me his pen to sign. My aunt took a pen out of her purse. "Honey, sign this," she said. "There is a wedding in four hours and a baby on the way."

I signed the contract and walked out of Steve's office a broken woman. I don't remember much else from that afternoon. I do remember Laura picked me up for my wedding. Jim had left earlier on his own. I was exhausted and sick. I told Laura everything in the car. When I got to the wedding, I put on my best game face, but my heart was broken. My father-in-law wanted to play the big-shot host, so I was limited as to the number of friends that I could invite to my own wedding. Between all their social friends and acquaintances and my family, we hit our maximum. I could only invite ten of my own friends. My wedding was a social occasion for my in-laws' friends and family, filled with people I did not know.

After we said our vows, my new husband made the rounds on his own. This was the first time in his family that the spotlight was on him, and he was ecstatic. I felt like I had strep throat or the flu but did not complain. I looked serene and happy, and I shook everyone's hand and smiled.

I was the supreme actress that night and kept that wonderful act going for years. The night of our wedding was unseasonably warm outside. Every time I made my way outdoors for a breath of fresh air, Jim or his parents would derail me with an obligatory introduction to some-one notable to the Fisher crew. They wanted me to pay homage to the big shots of the Chicago scene. My family never got to spend time with me that night and we all felt terrible about that.

I often have a dream where I am stopped from being with my loved ones in a beautiful setting, much like that wedding day. So many of those people I loved and who knew the real me are now gone. My mom, my aunt, my cousin, my sister-in-law—gone, no longer in my world. That moment we were all together, when I could have enjoyed them, was squandered while I had to play the smiling fool.

Jim's corporate attorney, the one who helped him execute that hateful contract, was a guest at my wedding. Tall, handsome, and suntanned, he stood smiling at me as I walked down the aisle. I could not have many of my dear friends at that event, but the bastard who denied me my marital rights and money was right there, front and center!

I was relieved when the night ended. We climbed into the limo to go downtown to stay at a hotel. I convinced myself from that day on to forget the details of the last month and focus on being the best wife and mother I could be.

The day after that, my new husband went on a golf trip, excited to be included by "the guys" and he insisted that I would be wrong to make him feel bad for leaving me so soon after our wedding. I swallowed my pride and said I was fine with it. I went out with my closest friends that first night and enjoyed myself more than I ever had with Jim.

Thirty days later, my mother went into the hospital for tests and died the same night, with my Aunt Myrna beside her. My mother had been ecstatic to learn I was carrying a little boy, and that fact kept her happy in those final weeks.

I was lost.

Four months later, my aunt returned from California to see the birth of my first baby, Ross, and help take care of him. I buried myself in Ross and felt the joy of falling in love with my new baby.

I had grown up bearing witness to a loveless marriage, and I assumed marriage was never easy or euphoric. I settled in to make the best of my situation. It never felt right, though, and I never felt content or truly happy. I had tried to marry someone safe, and ironically, he was the least safe choice I could have made.

That is my biggest regret. Women do themselves a disservice when they settle. Wait until it's right or cut your losses early. I often feel that the inner turmoil I felt ended up weakening me physically. I lost sight of what I wanted or needed and took what I thought was the path of least resistance.

It was abundantly clear that the two of us were absolutely, fundamentally incompatible. I was never genuinely happy, but we had our son and daughter quickly. I was three months pregnant with Ross at our wedding, and then came Sloan eighteen months later.

Jim continued to be selfish and demanding. I was plagued by disappointment in who he was as a father, husband, and human being, but true to form, I never shared this with anyone. I tried to convince myself and others that he was a bigger and better person than he really was.

I wanted a strong family unit for my two babies, so I threw myself into family life. I tried to create the best one I could, but it was never warm and cozy or fun and easy. Instead, it was stressful and nerve-wracking. I constantly felt Jim's judgement, and I became sensitive about his family's opinions, too.

Not long after we married, we moved to one of the suburbs outside Chicago, opting for the size of the house over its location. That decision quickly became polarizing. My best girlfriends still lived and worked in the city, and I was a retired fashionista, part-time realtor and full-time suburban mommy, light years away from my previous glamorous life.

Not only was I quickly and unceremoniously removed from that whole life and who I was as a person, my new mommy friends had no interest in hearing about any of my life story. It was a relic of the past. I tried to bury it, as it was no longer relevant, but losing that side of myself made me sad and numb.

I struggled to be a good cook and housekeeper in my new country club, suburban life. Instead of attending fabulous dinner parties with interesting people from all over the world, I now felt chastised for my lack of planning play dates or not knowing the merits of a particular toy.

Since my mother's passing, my Aunt Myrna, whom I absolutely idolized, had become my lifeline. She lived in Las Vegas near her two sons' families and my brother, Scott. Myrna taught me how to care for my newborn son. She was my rock, surrogate mother, and best friend, all rolled into one. I depended on her wisdom and love.

During my second pregnancy, my water broke prematurely at twenty-eight weeks. I had to remain perfectly still in the hospital so that my amniotic fluid would not drain out, causing an early birth. Finally, after prolonged contractions and bleeding, our perfect daughter arrived. My first call went to Aunt Myrna, my de facto mother, my aunt and close friend, but she had passed away from a cancer that had ravaged her body just hours before the birth. I pushed back my grief to focus on my newborn and toddler and saved my blues for another day.

Many women give up pieces of themselves when they marry and become mothers. In my case, my career as a clothing designer had to go on hold. Showrooms were closing in Chicago and fewer design jobs were available anywhere. In fact, they are usually few and far between because demand far outweighs supply in this field. Most people open a fashion company so they can design, and they rarely like sharing the limelight. My business did well critically, but like most creative start-ups it failed miserably on the business end.

I transitioned into real estate sales, which were booming in Chicago's suburbs. It can be a flexible and profitable career for a woman, but all the paperwork involved and dealing with other people's property didn't fit my skill set.

I had always been respected for my talent, creativity, humor, and intelligence. Now, I had a husband who complained about my housekeeping skills. I was a fish out of water in the suburbs and living with someone lacking in warmth and understanding.

I threw all my love and attention into my babies. What I lacked in actual mommy skills I made up for in my undivided love and attention. But as a new mother in a prosperous North Shore suburb, I felt constantly judged for not being a well-organized, do-it-all, super mom.

Within a few years, I began taking antidepressants, which zoned me out and kept me functional but numb. I knew this was not the real me and that I wasn't being true to myself, but I didn't know what to do about it.

Chapter Six:
Sickness

"No man or woman born, coward or brave, can shun his destiny." —Homer

I was feeling a little sick during the week leading up to Thanksgiving, 2008, but a slight sore throat and a few chills did not keep me from celebrating with my family in California.

I have always taken pride in my healthy lifestyle. Doctors claimed that if it weren't for my fitness when I got sick, I would have had no chance of survival. But how did a seemingly healthy woman fall so hard and so fast? Finding answers has been elusive.

My mother had claimed I was born with a lemon of a body, always fighting health issues as a girl. Every six weeks or so I would get a brutal cold or fever that would last weeks and turn into a chronic bronchial cough. This happened so frequently and lasted so long that I just forged ahead and lived my life. I grew tired of resting instead of enjoying time with my friends.

As an adult, I treated any initial signs of congestion as an allergy. I would try to dry out with neti pots and antihistamines before an infection could flare up. I loaded up on various vitamins and probiotics as well. I still got slammed with frequent and voracious colds.

When I got sick that Thanksgiving week, it started like most of the other bad head colds. I forged ahead till I just couldn't. I guess some people are born with weaker immune systems.

Every time I went to a new manicurist, they showed concern for the fungus under my nails. Everyone had a theory and a remedy. The last person said I should see a doctor and try to get rid of it, that it was not a good general sign. I did think something ugly could come from it one day, but little did I know that a regular Armageddon was headed my way.

The day after Thanksgiving, despite a slight stomachache and nausea, I joined everyone for dinner. Later that night, as the final credits of *Into the Wild* rolled across the TV screen, I was overcome with unexpected emotion and spent most of that night perspiring heavily and shaking with cold. When my fever spiked to 104.5, Jim took me to a critical care clinic. In the instant clinic, staff assessed my condition and said I had to be immediately transported to a hospital emergency room. At the critical care clinic, they said, "You are dying, and we are sending you by ambulance to the ER."

As I was being put inside the ambulance my husband told me he was going to leave me on my own so he could go find someone to remove a splinter on his foot. I wish I were kidding but I am not.

In the ER, the young, handsome, and aloof doctor assured me I would be fine and had "nothing serious," and sent me back to our hotel. Jim had left me, and I had become delirious and unable to form thoughts or ideas. I badly needed an advocate. Instead, I was alone and at the mercy of strangers. This doctor had not only misdiagnosed me, he ignored me. I tried to object but was either not heard or simply not listened to. I went along with these two men and their unflinching opinions, just as I had been trained to do since my childhood. I obeyed them quietly despite knowing it was so wrong. I stumbled out of the hospital trying to keep up with my husband who wanted out of there.

I slept fitfully for hours from the morphine I had received. So began a lengthy odyssey that may have been avoided if doctors recognized that I had been stricken with toxic shock syndrome, caused by group strep A bacteria in my bloodstream.

How does one get toxic shock? It's a condition which attacks your body, shutting down your organs and poisoning your blood stream. I somehow contracted a rare and lethal disease called Group Strep A, or Streptococcus A, which strikes infrequently, but is usually fatal. It is a time-sensitive bacterial infection that can be treated with early intervention antibiotics. The fact that it went so far and deep is where the tragedy lies. If I had been treated with standard medical care like IV antibiotics, the odds of my suffering limb loss and months of life support would have been much less. It was severe medical negligence, which much later a judge declared as the ultimate verdict.

Instead of getting appropriate treatment, less than twenty-four hours later, I was on life support in a medically induced coma, fighting a plethora of illnesses while trapped in an altered consciousness of dreams, visions, and hallucinations, including many I still vividly recall.

On a frigid snowy night, my comatose body was flown home to a Chicago hospital, unrecognizable to the friends who accompanied me, frozen in a silent scream with my mouth open, like the Munch masterpiece, with my hands and legs twisted like petrified wood. My soul was wandering. I dreamed that my friends were speaking about someone they knew who was extremely sick. I tried to speak up, but I was invisible to them, even as I realized they were speaking of me. I tried to tell them, but they didn't hear or see me. I simply did not exist.

As my family said their final goodbyes, I was deep in a coma with barely any chance of survival, teetering in another world, time traveling, and trying to find my way. My friend Jackie read to me from a book about John Lennon. In my dreamlike state, I remember listening to her melodic voice reading a chapter. I somehow felt like I was a part of that story. I was enraptured by a description of a person whose inner and outer beauty radiated goodness; a person who was deeply loved and admired by everyone around. Somehow I held on to those words, enjoying this exquisite tale.

As I listened, I envisioned myself walking through ordinary white gates, the kind of entrance similar to that leading to a quaint English village. I was walking down this lovely path on my way through the gates, feeling ecstatic and light. Since my recovery, I have scanned the John Lennon book and could not find any paragraph like what I saw and heard.

That was the last time for a long time that I would feel at peace and happy.

My next memory was being in a dark place, unmoving, where I was frozen in space. A man came in and asked me if Penny Fisher was there.

"I am here," I said.

He snapped his fingers and flames erupted. In that moment, I woke up.

I believe that is when I nearly died, coming as close as one possibly can without literally going. Once I had that vision, and something inside me recognized it, I had to come back to the surface. I was submerged under a coma state. My last memory as a whole person was being wheeled into the hospital, stuck in a freezing maze of pain, and altered consciousness, trying to communicate through a curtain of life and death.

Over the next several months, my internal organs faced repeated shutdowns and crashes, which triggered an excruciating series of surgeries to repair limbs and amputate others and set into motion years of painful recoveries.

When I finally awoke after seventy-five days, my first memory was the sound of my husband's trademark monotone, asking endless questions:

"What's your name? What are the kids' names? WAKE UP!"

The next voice I heard was a distant trace of my own, asking where I was and why my hands and feet were charcoal black. I could barely speak. I had tubes coming from my trachea, and I sounded like an alien. I could not understand why Jim was asking me stupid questions about my name and the names of our children.

Barely able to open my eyes, I saw big black claws, which I didn't recognize as my hands and feet. I thought it was a terrible nightmare. I asked about the rat growing beside me and visions of black claws. My sister-in-law Pam assured me there were no rats in the hospital.

This was the first time I realized where I was. As soon as I saw tubes coming from my throat and connected to my belly button, I forced myself back to sleep, hoping I could stay that way forever and avoid the reality waiting for me.

After repeatedly passing out and waking up, I moved my head, triggering an explosion of pain. I tried to scream but my throat was still blocked. All I could see through the open slits of my eyes were a group of doctors and nurses hovering over me and the shadows of Jim and members of my family, looking at me as if I were a horrible robot, terribly lost and damaged.

Stop staring!

But I couldn't speak.

My family explained that I had been "sleeping" in a coma because of toxic shock syndrome, which triggered other symptoms and life-threatening conditions. The good news was, I was back—sane, safe, and maybe sound—with my loved ones supporting me. The bad news was I had some limbs that were no longer alive.

I heard whispers about my fingers and the word "amputation" thrown around. As I came out of my extended sleep, a pair of doctors stopped by. My bed covers were off, and I noticed how the young, handsome doctor looked away immediately. This puzzled me because I smiled at him, or tried to, but he seemed ashamed to look at me.

I didn't know it at the time, but I was a living corpse, a skeleton with no hair and dead, black fingers and feet! No wonder he couldn't look! Beyond my naturally slim shape, I had lost fifty pounds.

An older doctor, Dr. Pearse, was wonderful. He looked at me kindly, with great warmth, which made me feel feminine, human, and cared for, something I desperately needed. He called me "Kiddo" and became my lifeline, a grandfatherly surgeon who made me feel like things could improve, repeatedly telling me, "The body is a wonderful machine and can do some incredible healing."

Chapter Seven:
Awakening

"Sleep, delicious and profound, the very counterfeit of death." —Homer

I tried to scream but couldn't. I thought no one heard me because they all ignored my wishes.

Hey Pam, Jim, somebody, hear me.

Nothing.

I need water! I just woke up from a very long nap and I'm thirsty!

I failed my first swallowing tests and would not be allowed any water, let alone solid food, until I passed. My status didn't change during the next three weeks, which exacerbated my suffering. I begged everyone who walked in and tried to trick them into giving me a drink. I didn't know there was a sign outside, warning everyone not to give me any liquids. I persisted, but no one folded, as each visitor put a sponge to my lips, like holy communion. I tried to suck, but even that was not allowed.

"Water . . ." I croaked. They must not hear me since everyone ignored my wishes. *Hey Pam, Jim, hello? I NEED WATER.*

I wanted to suck little ice chips but that wasn't allowed either. Three more weeks!

Eventually, I passed the barium test and could have water. I was given barium to swallow with dry crackers—disgusting food after starving for so long.

My next challenge was to start eating solid food. I needed to eat 1600 calories a day for three weeks before I could get the feeding tube in my stomach removed.

The entire process became a series of difficult tests, one after another, with tiny but meaningful prizes if I passed. My first prize was to have a sip of water, something I took for granted every day before my illness. When I was able to finally drink, I couldn't get enough of it. At the time, eating meant nothing, but quenching my thirst felt like I had reached a holy state of nirvana.

All mirrors were removed. I was not to see myself during any phase of my healing. My looks had been the one thing I was always told I had going for me. I wasn't a great student or athlete in my youth, but I was attractive in a way people noticed.

Who knew I would lose the one thing I felt good about? When you are challenged with loss, you develop other ways to cope and to establish your identity.

I could do nothing on my own, not eat, talk, or even breathe unassisted. I had a colostomy bag and a feeding tube connected to me. I tried to talk but since I was intubated, it sounded mechanical.

Every day I faced impossible feats; things I used to take for granted like walking, talking, sitting, and standing were impossible for me in those early days of consciousness. It took superhuman strength, focus, and humility to get through everything, but I had to survive for the sake of my young children. They needed me to be there and help them grow into their own lives. I needed to try and recreate a happy life for us—I just didn't know how. But I was determined. I would also make myself beautiful again because that is how I felt within. I was an attractive, gregarious, fun, and loving mom, and I was damned if I couldn't at least try to be that way again.

Trying to make a full recovery without the use of my hands or feet was like being lost in the ocean with no boat and no direction home. I tried to stay in the present and not overthink the future, an exercise of sheer will. I was determined to make a complete comeback despite missing my extremities. I tried to count my blessings and not focus on the horror, but it was difficult. The constant love and visitations from friends and family kept me from the darkness that could have easily engulfed me.

—◊—

"Penny! Wake up!"

I was laid out flat in my hospital bed, just days after coming out of my three-month coma, when I heard a familiar, wonderfully crass voice urging me to rejoin the living.

"Penny! Did you notice I lost fifteen pounds on SlimFast?"

Jackie Derchact was shouting from across my room in the ICU.

Can't say that I have.

Jackie Eisenberg had been parked at my bedside for a while, gently caressing my arm and humming softly to me. We were both jolted by Jackie Dercacht's invasion of our space, but that was just Jackie being Jackie, a long-time, loving, caring friend.

I tried to enjoy her new appearance but since I still suffered from diminished eyesight and saw double, I couldn't appreciate Jackie's new body. She either looked twice as big as I remembered, or her new slim version just kept shifting in front of me. I tried to keep my eyes open and enter some level of jovial consciousness, but as Jackie Eisenberg continued holding my hand, I fell quickly back to sleep.

The next day—I think—I was awakened by a loud, clomping noise coming from the corridor and coming closer to my room. That must be Christina. After being in a deep slumber for three months I could still recognize Christina's footsteps! As she entered the room, my eyes detected a shiny glimmer of gold. In all that time, my eyes had barely seen a ray of light.

"What is that?" I groaned.

"Oh, these are my new Tory Burch shoes!" Christina said, as if we were meeting in a shopping mall. "Aren't they cute?"

She held up a six-inch heel for my review.

"What day is it?" I asked.

"Sunday, silly," she said.

"Is that what you wear to a hospital on a Sunday afternoon?" I croaked, still quite hoarse from not having spoken since what felt like forever.

Christina started to shake, which she always does when a laugh is beginning in her belly. She is another of my absolute best friends, a character, and a riot to be around.

Then Jackie Eisenberg walked in.

"Did Jackie Dercacht really wake me from the dead to ask if I noticed her fifteen-pound weight loss?"

Jackie nodded, and the three of us erupted in laughter. Well, I didn't exactly erupt. I must have whimpered and tried to maintain a smile.

I thanked God for that moment—and still do—particularly because Jackie and Christina later shared how they were afraid I would never laugh again. I had not yet shown any emotion since my re-entry to earth, nothing happy or sad or in between, because I was still in such shock and disbelief that I even existed.

But this laughter, this beautiful, recognizable laughter in my hospital room broke the spell. I began to feel hope.

I woke up to a full heart despite being physically demolished, because so many of my old friends were near and visiting me often. I had been lonelier than I cared to admit in my sad marriage. Having my beloved friends around made me realize how deeply loved and important

I was to so many people. In my unhappy marriage, I had all but forgotten my own personal value.

As I recovered, I realized I was more than my looks. I had to learn my own true value. Although I was no longer pretty on the outside, my soul was deep, and I had meaningful relationships and love all around me. That nourished me enough to survive. I understood my worth more than ever before, and it was a revelation.

One night, alone in my hospital room a few months after regaining consciousness, a young doctor bluntly informed me that my infected limbs would have to be amputated. I had known I was in trouble, but no one had yet confirmed this overwhelming life sentence. Right then and there, I decided to not think about the news again until I had to. I went on chatting with my sister-in-law as if I barely had a care. I simply shut down that part of my brain. I found out what survival mode means. Staying numb kept me alive!

I loved my in-laws and had become very close to my father-in-law, who sometimes dished out little pearls of wisdom, such as not to think too far ahead, to just focus on one day at a time, one hour at a time, or minute to minute. I still live in the moment and try not to think too far ahead. It's helped me feel lighter and stay happier and enjoy where I am instead of stressing about the past or future.

I was awakened at four a.m. each morning to receive painful shots in my abdomen. I cried myself back to sleep, only to be awakened again in the gray, early morning light to receive my next round of meds and rehab. I had deep lesions on the back of my skull, so I couldn't lay on my back. I could barely lie on my side because my ribs protruded from being so emaciated. I could never lie on my stomach because I was attached to so many tubes, one for feeding, another for eliminating, and one for breathing.

It was hard to find a part of my body that didn't hurt. Even to this day I struggle to find a position of comfort.

Sometimes, I would ask whoever was visiting me to rub a small area in between my rib cage for relief but trying to sit up was painful and extremely challenging because my muscles had atrophied. A giant device helped me sit up so I could develop muscle strength, but I was shaken and weak. When I did sit, my stomach filled with fluid, making me look pregnant even though I was thin as a skeleton. My teeth hurt, my head was raw, and I was always nauseous and dizzy.

Pain was a constant.

I detail my difficulties not for pity but to explain how far I had to go to recover, not only physically but mentally, too. No matter how long the road would be, I was determined to have a good life, despite the humiliation I would have to endure. I would reinvent myself however I could, despite my new limitations. I had to play out the hand to the best of my ability, through a never-ending journey of love and determination.

I had visitors every day, which helped distract and comfort me. I had a workout schedule, but I always looked forward to getting back in bed to rest and hide. I loved having people around me, but my senses were so tapped out it hurt to talk or sit up. I was sensitive to sounds and light and found them difficult to manage for very long.

True to form, I always felt the need to be up for my guests, despite the constant pain. My only reprieve was when I slept, but the pain was there each time the staff woke me up for various shots and treatments.

When I had to go to the bathroom in the middle of the night, I pressed the call button and waited for a nurse to come and lift me into a wheelchair and transfer me onto the toilet. I was relieved when I was put back into my bed and the pillows around my bony body were rearranged. Once again, even for a minute, I could enjoy a tiny dose of comfort.

When I awoke from my coma, the first thing I wanted, besides water, was to see my children. I had to wait until I became fully lucid, and the respirator was removed from my throat. By then, I was desperate to see my babies. They were all I could think of, and it became my biggest motivation to get better.

Sloan had turned seven years old three months earlier, when I was in my coma. My friends had thrown her a birthday party at my house. Ross was only eight.

I wondered how they would be able to handle seeing their mother as a living cadaver. I had not yet seen myself in a mirror, so I didn't know how frighteningly sick and old I looked. My family tried to graciously help me put myself back together while keeping up my spirits.

The nurses thought my children were my grandchildren and my friends were my children. I was blissfully unaware of my looks and overlooked their confusion. That's the mother that Sloan and Ross were seeing for the first time since Thanksgiving of 2008. Maybe if I had seen myself, I would have hidden myself away.

I've always thought I am the luckiest woman in the world to have such beautiful children. When I went for an ultrasound during my second pregnancy, I was already on cloud nine because of my amazing son. Having a girl to complete the family was a dream. I still think my mother-in-law paid that nurse to tell me I was having a girl, as if she and my mother were sending me an angel, a divine spirit of warmth and goodness. Because when that nice nurse told us we were having a girl we screamed so loud and for so long that the nurses kindly shut the door and left us alone in our euphoria.

Ross became my partner in crime from the moment he was born. I took him everywhere with me. I wanted him to experience every angle of light and every event worth noting, from restaurants to museums and long walks around Lake Michigan. He coolly absorbed it all with a great sense of humor and a keen eye for observation.

When Sloan would crawl into my lap and look at me with her enormous green eyes and hug me for what seemed like forever, I wanted to stay like that, heart to heart, cozy and comfy, extending our personal moment for as long as possible.

—⁓—

When the kids entered my hospital room, Sloan went straight to a table and began coloring on a piece of scrap paper. She later told me it was so she didn't have to see me. It became her coping mechanism.

Ross came in and immediately moved some wires from the machines and life support tubes surrounding me and laid down next to me on my narrow hospital bed, barely big enough to hold a child.

The contact I felt was the most delicious thing a human being can ever experience. Besides being incessantly probed by a team of doctors and nurses, this was a loving, genuine touch. I think Jim had been too scared to touch me for fear of killing me. Having Ross so close was pure ecstasy.

Then he sat up and stared at my head, which was bald except for a trace of bangs in the front. I had massive bedsores all over the back of my head from not moving for so many months.

"Hey Mom, I like your hair. It makes your big eyes even bigger." I barely believed him, but it was sweet for him to say.

Ross accepted that I was alarmingly thin and still quite sick, but Sloan never came back to the hospital because she was too scared and upset by my appearance. My heart still breaks, imagining what they went through for more those three months, not knowing if their mother would ever return from those mysterious hospitals, forbidden to see me for so long because they were too young, and I was too sick.

What happens to young children who are naturally attached to their mother when she disappears one night with no explanation? What does that do to a child's deepest sense of security and trust?

From the moment I was first hospitalized in California, Ross and Sloan were understandably kept away and little information was provided to them. In fact, little was known about my survival. Their father wasn't home to comfort them, either; he had stayed back to wait it out. We had various family coming in to take care of them, but they were traumatized and scared by our absence.

Sloan was so sad I missed her birthday party that year, she still talks about it to this day. I was touched by my best friends' kindness and thoughtfulness in making it nice for her and bringing her a sense of normalcy in such an abnormal time. I cannot say enough about my lifelong friends Laura, Alissa, Christina, and Jackie. For their friendship alone, I am a truly blessed woman.

Throughout the waiting, before they were allowed to see me, Ross held in his emotions and became quiet and withdrawn. Sloan was shaken, even more when she would see her friends with their moms. She didn't understand why she couldn't have *her* mom. My friends and family visited frequently to comfort the kids, but it was all difficult and sad.

Ross visited every Saturday and always told me how nice he thought I looked, and I came to believe him. Sloan called me every day. I still didn't realize how scary I looked with everything else I had to focus on. While I understood Sloan's feelings, after a few more weeks, I couldn't bear the separation any longer. My friends and I hatched a plan to improve my appearance and put me in a less intimidating environment. We found a wig maker and had her expedite making me a clip-on hairpiece. It was difficult to attach to my bangs and quite painful, but it worked! I then had to gain ten pounds, which was no easy task as I had a tiny shrunken stomach and could not hold down much food. It was like having intense morning sickness, but I gained the weight even though eating made me feel wretched for a long time after. I never would have realized how challenging it could be to gain weight, but it felt like torture.

Just one of many obstacles to overcome.

After bandaging my hands and feet so my necrotic skin wouldn't show and clipping on the wig, I had the nurses dress me in semi-cute sweats and my sister-in-law put me in full makeup. I finally looked human enough for my daughter to see me, so off we went.

It was a cold winter night as Jim wheeled me down the street to our friends Tricia and Paul's house near the hospital.

When we got there, we put my wheelchair away and I sat on a couch looking somewhat normal, but Sloan still refused to look at me. She wouldn't leave the bathroom. It was horrifying and heartbreaking. After several hours, I tricked her by playfully asking to see a tooth she had lost. She reflexively turned toward me and lit up when she saw I was her same mommy. She ran to me, showering me with hugs and kisses. Our reverie lasted long enough to warm my soul.

This felt like the beginning of the long road home.

It felt odd being out of my insulated hospital room that day, as though I had been released from prison, feeling unsure of freedom and if I could ever exist in the real world. It was destabilizing.

Chapter Eight:
Rehabilitation

"Go on with a spirit that fears nothing" —Homer

As I came back to the living, I remember being scrubbed down by several different hospital staff members. I couldn't see them, but I felt them washing me. I always croaked out a "thank you," no matter what. One time someone was too rough when they scrubbed me; I believe it was a male nurse but at that time I was still in a fog. I began to weep and heard my sister-in-law ask why I was crying. Then she understood.

"Too rough?"

I nodded and cried myself back into a deep sleep.

In four hospitals over six months, I met incredible, caring nurses; but I had one who seemingly chose the wrong profession. One night, "Nurse Ratchet" ignored my rings for help and seemed to revel in her power. All I could do was scream and cry. Finally, my father-in-law registered a complaint and I never saw her again. She was one bad apple among many wonderful nurses who cared for me so lovingly for many months. They became my lifeline, and I came to respect them deeply.

Some were religious and sang to me. Some stayed with me through the night. I never doubted my ability to recover and become my old self again. And I did, but it was a long, hard road back, and the nurses helped to make it possible.

Sitting in my wheelchair, I used to try willing people to see who I really was so they could recognize the beauty I felt inside. They would often respond with kindness and respect rather than pity, which was important to me, and I appreciated it.

To say that living in a wheelchair is humbling and exhausting is a gross understatement. I have met many wonderful people who live permanently like that, and they still lead full, productive lives. That said, my short-term goal was to free myself from the wheelchair. I was recovering for months in a rehab institute, on a floor that was predominantly serving paraplegics.

I have learned that some people will always have an easier time in life than you but so many have it far worse. I was one of the lucky ones who would eventually be able to shed my wheelchair and walk again independently but looking at my black hands and feet I could not even imagine how I ever could or would. But I remained eager and focused.

During those early days, I was like a soldier, awakening each day to my new reality. I was serious and stoic and had no idea how I would ever smile again. I was a bald warrior with terrible scars, devoid of my usual personality. It took a long time for me to share my first laugh but thankfully I did and quickly learned the value of humor as a tool of survival and positive communication.

Years later, when I went back to that rehabilitation center, many of the nurses did not recognize me until I explained who I was, the corpse who came back to life. I felt like the count of Monte Cristo, very Machiavellian, in my new disguise of normalcy. In many ways, I still feel like that every day: I look like a normal, healthy, happy person, yet I have so much more going on underneath the surface.

After regaining some of my eyesight, balance, and clarity, I went about the business of recovering. I needed to literally shed the different life-supporting apparatuses that had kept me alive in those darker days. The doctors had me pass tests by going through various protocols to graduate to the next level.

For example, while I was in the third hospital, they removed the tracheal tube out of my throat as soon as I proved I could breathe on my own. In the fourth hospital, I was required to eliminate on my own. To accomplish this, I needed to strengthen my body to withstand sitting unassisted. After being in a coma, lying virtually still for three months, my muscles had atrophied, with little to no muscle left.

Each day, I sat up a tiny bit longer, in increments of seconds. Each second caused unbearable discomfort and exhaustion. I needed to lie back down immediately. After a few weeks, though, I could sit up for five straight minutes! I was ready to sit on a toilet and eventually sit on a chair in a shower.

Finally, I was able to shed the urine bag attached to my leg. I had even gone to my workout sessions with that thing swishing around my leg. Every day for four hours I was placed on a cushion to do various leg, arm, and stomach exercises. It was tough, but not as bad as the battle of trying to eat again. I needed to digest my food to recover, but eating was repugnant at first and it was difficult to keep the food down. But doing so was essential to my final graduation. I needed to gain twenty pounds to leave the hospital and rid myself of my feeding tube. Eventually, after many weeks of trying, and after no solid food for four months, I had the smelly and painful feeding tube removed, which required morphine because the pain was so great.

Each time I needed to use the bathroom, I rang for a nurse and waited for them to come. They would carry me on their back to a wheelchair and take me to the bathroom and carry me to the toilet. One night, a new nurse promised to come right away. I waited for over an hour. I was so upset I called Jim, who had to come back and calm me. My blood pressure had gotten dangerously high because I was so upset.

The regular nurses were mostly wonderful, one in particular whose name was Betty. Betty treated me as if I were her own child and I am forever grateful for her care and devotion.

Others were sadly lacking in compassion or a nurturing bedside manner, especially one doctor. At this time, my necrotic black foot had a portion of healthy ankle skin. I was allowed to push lightly on that quarter of my ankle but was warned that any pressure could result in my foot falling off. "She can only touch this area of her heel for a quick transfer to her wheelchair," the compassionless doctor had said.

I tried to understand exactly how I was supposed to climb down from a tall hospital bed without the use of my other foot or hands and land gently on that quarter-sized area on my heel to quickly pivot onto my wheelchair. When I asked the doctor how I could do it, he finally spoke directly to me after months of talking about me in the third person. He glared at me through his black, horned-rimmed glasses. "If you don't land exactly on that area, and only that area, your foot can self-amputate, and we don't want that now do we, Ms. Fisher?"

I had always been flexible, both physically and mentally, but this was a trying feat for anyone in the world to master, much less a sick, drugged, ninety-pound patient trying to attend a physical therapy session after laying still and immobile for three months. Demanding that I hit the "bullseye" was daunting, much less facing the prospect of my foot falling off.

A few days after surgery, when they cut away more of my foot, I was balanced on one knee on a scooter, hopping down the hospital hallway on a plastic leg, pushing up my glasses, while trying to protect my partial fingers. Using the scooter with one hand and pushing my glasses up with the other means my fingers kept falling off. It was a comedy of errors, an absurd piece of performance art.

The first time I was hoisted in a wheelchair into a van, avoiding pressure on my foot made me look as if I were paralyzed. When I ended up with burning pain in my foot, I threw up and pretended I was fine. On that day, like many others, I resolved to not live like a victim. I made a promise that day that no matter how much pain and discomfort I had to privately endure, I would not let them see me sweat—ever.

—⟋⟍—

My kids were elated when I was finally able to come back home. They spent most of their time around me while I was recovering enough strength to withstand the unavoidable—all the major surgery I would have to endure. It wound up being less than two months before I had to go back in the hospital for major and brutal surgery.

The doctors had suggested doing each amputation separately, first one leg below the knee, then a partial foot, and finally seven more fingers. Since each procedure would require an eight-week recovery before even thinking about fitting into prosthetics, I opted to do the surgeries together, to go for it all at once. I would just rip off the Band-Aid and take lots of pain medication, and then I would be done. Either way I knew it would be painful, so why not just go for it and get my mobility back as soon as possible? Why prolong the anguish? Besides, it was abhorrent any way I looked at it.

I tried to turn my brain off and coast through the tough times, but that simply wasn't possible. When it came to surgery and the recovery period, there would be no coasting through anything, no shortcuts.

I was scared. The day before, Pam came to spend what we thought would be a quiet, intimate day together. Then my doorbell rang and a lovely and fun group of eight girlfriends sauntered in with soup and wine to surprise me with a party. We played music and giggled and didn't think too much about the following day.

I slept for several days after the surgery because sleep has always been my ultimate escape. On one of my first nights post-surgery, a young sweet-faced resident asked if he could sit with me. He wanted to ask about where I got my strength and positive attitude. He had observed the pictures that my friends tacked to my wall and saw me smiling and laughing with them when they came to visit. He wondered how I kept smiling.

I told him two things: faith and love all around me. Those were the two forces that pulled me through. I felt much more connected to the universe after my near-death experience. The person I had been before never really made it out of the ER that day. I was reborn months later and miles away, in a strange hospital, bald and emaciated and as helpless as a newborn chick with yellowed, hairless skin.

The young doctor and I sat in silence until the sun came through the dreary blinds, and then we wished each other well. He was such a kind young man with great intentions. I'm sure he became a fine doctor with his gentleness and empathy, unusual for a doctor his age or any age for that matter. At least according to my experience with doctors.

Photos

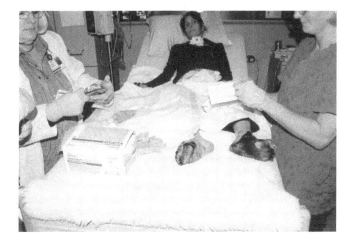

I wake up from the three-month coma with charcoal black extremities. Hard to look at.

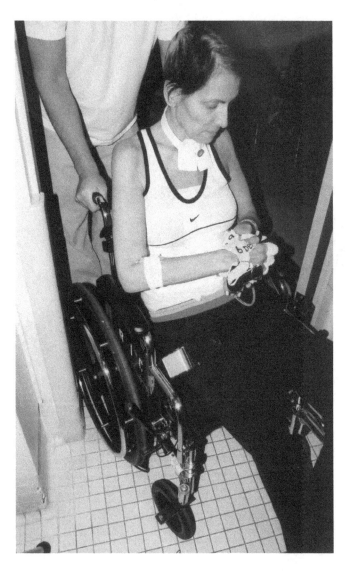

A week after waking up from the coma, muscles atrophied, unable to walk, still shocked and feeling overwhelmed and hopeless.

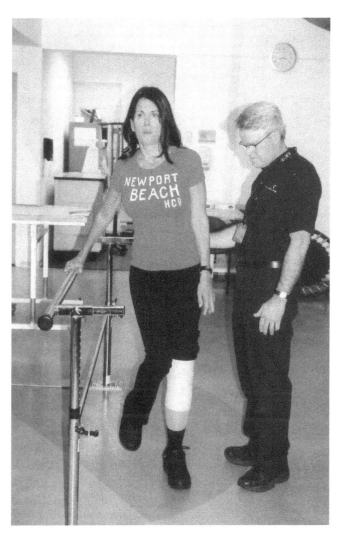

Eight weeks post coma. Walking out of there with my wig on.

Three months post surgery volleying tennis balls. Beautiful hair extensions.

Recent boxing lesson.

The kids and I in Malibu, Thanksgiving, 2019.

Chapter Nine.
Walking Again

"Be strong saith my heart; I am a soldier; I have seen worse sights than this." —Homer

My first day with a new prosthetic didn't go well. Initial prosthetics are big, ugly, and heavy because patients quickly outgrow their starter versions. My insurance company tried to avoid paying for any leg whatsoever by declaring a prosthetic leg a luxury and not a necessity. I imagine if they or their loved ones happened to lose their own mobility, they would know the necessity of replacing a lost leg.

This was just one of many injustices I suffered at the hands of insurance companies and frauds. I also had sub-par resources to rely on for emotional help. The hospital where I recovered never followed through on introducing me to other experienced amputees. One of my surgeons drily explained that anyone who had my experience was dead, so he had nobody to offer. This attitude made me feel like I was living on the moon, alone and desolate. Later, through my own personal research and acquaintances, I met the leader of a charity called Adaptive Adventures and this organization became my touchstone.

The first day I tried to walk caused heartbreaking pain and frustration. I could not bear to think about this heavy, exhausting, painful weight functioning as a stand-in leg.

Nothing would ever be easy, carefree, and natural again. When the truth came crashing down on me that day, I felt a total loss of control. I couldn't shake off the grief; my heart was broken. I had to come to terms with my new life, but I could not see how.

Pam took me home and tried to comfort and soothe me but even she, who had always been my rock, couldn't get through. My heart felt irreparably shattered. I now understood the meaning of a broken heart.

However, no matter how hopeless things seemed, I vowed to survive. I had to for my children; I could never leave them without putting up a fight. And fight I did, for what seemed like twenty-four hours a day.

During my final fitting appointment, the prosthetist had me stand by a set of parallel bars to walk just a few steps. He then stepped out to grab my release form. In that time, I began walking around the room and then out into the hallway, where I continued down a long corridor into an elevator and out of the hospital! That doctor was quite shocked to see me walking at such a speed.

It was sheer determination on my part because each step felt like trudging through cement. I was wet with sweat and with the effort, pain, and strain of this Herculean feat. I needed to do this if I was ever going to feel normal again. I needed to walk freely, unencumbered by a walker or even a cane. It often feels like I'm walking on burning coals because of the tissue damage; but I breathe through it and keep walking—putting one foot in front of the other, propelling myself forward, always hopefully forward.

My right foot creates a lot of the problem. If it were just one or the other, it might be more doable, but the combination of both makes walking incredibly challenging. Yet there are many hours and even days where I feel like myself and not altered in any way. But then, something always brings me back to the reality of my limits; every move I make leaves me vulnerable to accidents. I hated feeling helpless and unreliable back then, and I still do.

Eight weeks is the minimum required time after an amputation for your skin to heal and survive before you can be fitted for prosthetics, let alone how long it can take until you can walk again after being in a wheelchair.

Artificial legs can cost between $10,000 and $25,000, depending on the materials used. Many amputees have multiple models. I have only one because it was so expensive, but it's beautiful and looks incredibly real, which makes me comfortable. Many amputees, especially athletes, use highly creative and aerodynamic models.

It takes a lot of visits to get the fit right. The process is painful and time consuming, as you often must wait all day during numerous fittings and adjustments. They make the prosthetics on-site, and adjust them to fit, with a lot of trying on, redoing, adjusting, and refitting.

Two days after I received my leg, which was ten weeks post-surgery, I put on a white linen shirt and pants and went to watch tennis at our country club with my friends Jacki and Danielle. A woman sitting near us overheard our conversations about what I'd just come through. She confessed that when she saw me come in, she had assumed I was just another fortunate mom. She said she would have to think twice about judging someone based on appearances.

I was still so new at walking again that I constantly tested my capabilities. That day, I walked out on the tennis court and volleyed with my friend Danielle. She snapped a picture I'm quite proud of, looking fierce and strong holding a racket, my long hair extensions glowing sleek in the sun.

"So, Mom," Ross said in his usual mature manner, "what are you unable to do that you have done before? You've played tennis, rode your bike, swam, and done yoga. There's nothing you can't do! Let's keep a checklist of your challenges and write down all your accomplishments overcoming them."

This was my now nine-year-old boy, so positive and logical, who taught me such valuable life lessons. Despite how introspective and introverted he had seemed to become, perhaps for his own protection, I think Ross made it through this well. It's sometimes hard to know with a young boy, but today he is a successful young man.

Sloan, on the other hand, who endured such sadness and uncertainty, took more time to return to normal. I am sure my condition took whatever adolescent issues she had to a whole new level, and she had to develop a thick skin to make it through such a hurtful and uncertain time. As I watched her manage, growing tall and fit, she came into her own as a breathtaking beauty with contact lenses, sculpted eyebrows, and lovely skin. But her real appeal is in her poise, serenity, and kindness.

Seeing Ross and Sloan overcome the trauma of nearly losing their mother to become confident, mature young adults, I couldn't be prouder or more relieved.

The day after that tennis game, Ross and I decided to go for a bike ride. Again, I pushed my boundaries. I went on an eleven-mile bike ride in untested shoes to show off my resilience, and I paid dearly for it.

The top of my foot swelled and turned purple, due to an infection in my supporting bone. It was not only terribly painful, but threatened the survival of my existing foot and my overall health. A global infection like that could derail my recovery.

I was never sure if this infection was dormant in my foot, and the bike ride exposed it or if a foreign body infected my foot from my shoe rubbing against it. This was a major setback that overwhelmed my life for many years. I not only had to sustain three more surgeries, but I also had to get blood transfusions to build my immunity, wear a PICC line in my arm, and get hourly antibiotics drips. For a year I went in for hyperbaric oxygen treatments. At first the tank felt claustrophobic, but I came to enjoy the meditative solitude during those four hours a day, four days a week.

I bonded with the young, hip technician, a guy named Lance who was into classic alternative rock. He had a quick, sarcastic wit, which I loved to spar with; I came to look forward to those sessions. They energized me and provided a place of peace. Also, they did wonders for my hair and skin. Those treatments were my respite from the world. Eventually, I developed cataracts from the oxygen. I had them removed, one at a time. There is a one in a million chance of complication from cataract surgery, a rare disorder called epithelial downgrowth. Guess who got it.

This set off another wild goose chase into the medical abyss. Somehow, I'm still standing, and I still look and feel like myself. Somehow, I manage to eke out a little happiness, but it's hard won and never easy to sustain.

After the surgeries, I battled osteomyelitis for years, a powerful and destructive infection that raged in the main bone in my existing stump of a foot. No words for the pain, so let's not even try. My fourth and final surgery was done to strengthen the bone. The surgeon rebuilt my metatarsal with a putty solution, which was normally used by neurologists as a soft tissue filler.

There were many days I suffered from a general malaise. I was bone weary, faint-in-your-chair exhausted. How do you function when all you want to do is sleep? I could no longer remember ever having energy, ever feeling good or having a pain-free moment.

As I battled the powerful infection in my foot, my depression threatened to swallow me whole. I had my fair share of breakdowns, and when I felt inconsolable, I would indulge for several hours in my ultimate escape—sleep—when, at least initially, I was not an amputee in my dream world. Eventually, reality caught up and not even my dreams offered any escape from who I was.

Each day I looked to lift myself up, to be friendly and social by greeting people, to welcome their questions (no matter how stressful they were), and to show good humor and transparency even when they were judgmental. That's when I started my new mantra—fake it till you make it—as a means of surviving and bringing love into my life. To avoid depression, I forced myself to be friendly and social and to go out of my way to greet people. I did this until it felt sincere, but at first it was a forced effort. I felt like I needed to be with other people to fill a void, but people can be tiring and judgmental and full of advice about things they know nothing about.

Although I was walking and talking, the road to recovery was almost impossible to navigate. It took relentless dedication and focus and required extensive trial and error, which often brought great disappointment. So much time, money and patience pursuing the wrong pair of shoes or a prosthetic, but we didn't know better. We were in unchartered territory.

My sister-in-law Pam had found a medical artist on the Internet named Greg Gion. Jim took me there on a hot summer day before we were to meet our friends at the pool of our summer club.

Greg greeted us in his satellite office some twenty-five miles away. I was still wisp thin but beginning to look more fashionable than skeletal. I wore white jeans, a black t-shirt, and a giant black straw hat over my long wig. He seemed mildly surprised by the sight of me. I might have looked more glamorous than I felt. I was curious about what kind of people Greg met in his profession of reconstructing fingers and ears. Greg was lovely, a true artist with big, green, sensitive eyes and longish brown hair.

He deftly studied each of my fingers with trancelike intensity. I twitched in discomfort. My new prosthetic hurt to sit in, and the jeans were tight against the cast. My right foot was on fire, and I had to kick off that shoe.

Minutes turned into hours until we bid Greg goodbye and drove off into the hot sunlight to meet our friends. What should have been a thirty-minute ride turned into a bumper-to-bumper affair. Jim had the top down on his small sports car. I normally love the feel of a convertible and the wind in my hair and the sun on my face. But as we moved at a snail's pace, the hot sun went through my jeans and burned the rubber sleeve on my leg. I started to scream and swear and cry, which unsettled Jim, who had not seen me in such a state and was deeply affected by my moods. An hour later, we walked shakily into the pool area and to my girlfriends. They took one look and proceeded to soothe me with their loving empathy and understanding.

Eventually, I got my new fingers, the last piece of the puzzle, and they were a masterpiece, done with loving precision by Greg the perfectionist. It's rare to find someone of his skill and integrity. He was a wonderful doctor. Years later, my seven artificial fingers act as if they are autonomous creatures, with minds of their own.

—∭—

To save my foot, I took various cocktails of antibiotic IVs, administered multiple times a day by family and friends or worn as a patch for months on my right arm.

With the help of a healing counselor, I did an eight-month cleanse, which ridded my body of the toxic chemicals which had been administered to keep me alive. I still subscribe to a regimen of healthy eating and believe it is one of our best defenses against sickness. I found an innate ability to make the best of things, despite occasional bouts of deep depression.

Ten weeks following the surgery, my foot was healed enough to walk on, with the help of pain killers. As I slogged through that battle, I tried to rein in my marriage, but it takes two people. I thought Jim valued his family, but at home, he never lifted a helping hand without a fight.

Laying in my bed one day, exhausted from fighting for every crumb of what was left of our marriage, I spontaneously called my sister-in-law Pam and announced I was divorcing Jim. She was saddened but not surprised.

I was physically a mess, barely able to stay awake or function. I couldn't drive when these spells of fatigue came on, but I tried to keep it together for the family. I was determined to lead a productive and active life. I forced myself to exercise and often fell asleep on the floor during or after class. Once I felt the oxygen leave my body then blacked out. This was scary, and I fought to retain my energy, but getting much done was difficult.

I pushed myself unrealistically because I wasn't aware of the trauma to my body. I had been on full life support in a coma for three months. I didn't understand the carnage that had nearly destroyed me. I soldiered on, expecting to recover as if I had only endured a bad flu. My condition was more dire than I understood. I wanted to recover so badly that I kept thinking *mind over matter*. But some situations are irreversible and deadly serious, and this was both.

I told only a few close girlfriends about the debilitating pain and exhaustion. Up until then, I had hidden it from everyone, even from myself. The people living in the sheltered and affluent area where I was raising my family had not seen many amputees. They did not know how to react.

I wore a pain patch that slowly dripped a powerful narcotic. When I soaked in a hot tub, which gave me relief and comfort, I didn't realize the heat released the meds at once, giving me a double dosage and then depleting it for the next day. My body would be hungover from the dose, which meant I needed to detox.

It was difficult to get up with my kids, feed them, and get them off to school before going about my day. I pushed myself to get through it and then went to my group yoga class, where I would pass out at the end.

I tried working mornings for a cute boutique at a hair salon. I got so ill and fatigued, I would have to go to my car and lie down. Once or twice I went to throw up and passed out on my car during break. I tried, but I wasn't physically ready yet and had to quit.

I trained my mind to accept constant pain. I smiled and avoided complaining because it could bring everyone down. Anger and bitterness only compromised my dignity. I would not let pain defeat me. I didn't let it do that during the darkest days, and I won't allow it to now. This is a matter of pride for me, and a gift to my loved ones.

Chapter Ten:
On the Other Side of
the Looking Glass

"A man who has been through bitter experiences and trav-
elled far enjoys even his sufferings after a time" —Homer

I remember the first day when I felt like I was finally a
regular mom for Sloan.

"Mom, can you bring my dance shoes to school?"
Sloan asked sweetly on the phone. "I have Pom Squad
after school, and I can't cheer without them."

"Sure honey, I'll be right there," I told her, hoping my
frown didn't show through the phone. "But next time,
please make it easier on me and don't forget, okay?"

"Okay, Mom," she said sincerely. "Sorry."

If she only knew . . .

I had to become a suburban mommy all over again,
which meant showing up at ball games in a wig, smiling,
using a walker and/or hopping on one foot, loving the
chance to be around my children.

I'm a member of the stay-at-home mom sorority, and
while we usually have the time and opportunity to bring

a pair of dance shoes to school for their daughter, it's not always our first choice of activities. In most cases, it would be no trouble, but during winters in Chicago, which resemble an arctic vortex and seem to last most of the year, it's a test for me to pull off the ten- minute ride to Sloan's middle school without the very real threat of contracting gangrene in my bad foot, which is super susceptible to frostbite.

When Sloan called, I was lying on my bed, praying for pain relief. It was 20 degrees below zero, which meant with the wind chill factor, the temperature was probably unmentionable. I dragged myself off the bed and threw on my torture chamber of a boot. I took the chair stair down to the first floor, hobbled through the house into the ice-slicked garage, and climbed in my car. As soon as my hands touched the freezing steering wheel, they ignited in a firestorm of pain. It took forever for the heat in my car to kick in. Until that luscious moment arrived, I was afraid of the damage I might have done to my hands and my foot.

I pulled up at Sloan's school, but there was no parking! I couldn't walk outside to bring Sloan her shoes. I called her, but school rules wouldn't let her come outside. That made sense—for most of the world. I hailed down a friendly-looking teacher and begged her to take Sloan's shoes. She agreed. Yes! Mission accomplished.

"Thank you," I told her, wondering if she had any idea what a good deed she had just done.

By the time I got home, there was no chance to relax because Ross's basketball game began soon after. *Get it together, Penny!* Even in the best of times I was not exactly organized. Now, my mind gets stuck on pain and fatigue and keeping up with anything seems much harder. But that stuff doesn't matter. It just can't. As I entered the gym for Ross's game, I tried very hard to walk confidently and to smile. I realized that this was my chance to sit serenely on the steel bleachers and make small talk with other parents. A few lovely moms complimented me on how nice I looked. If they only knew! Inside, I was writhing in pain and discomfort. But it was time to be a mom, like any other mom, oblivious to my own agenda and concentrating solely on my kids.

—∿—

After making it through the molding of new fingers, adding hair extensions, getting a new leg, a foot brace and removing the film from over my eyes, I had to deal with a raging bone infection in my surviving partial foot. I tried to play it down, but my wound was oozing; and when I exerted myself, it would blow up and turn black and yellow on the inside. The skin was stretched so tight that the opening on top of my foot would fill up with puss and turn black. When I washed the area, the puss exploded in my face. The puss developed a mound of no less than three inches! It would throb and frighten me with the pain. After all the surgeries and treatments, now a chronic bone infection threatened to live forever in my partial, existing foot.

First, I took antibiotics, then I had an IV three times a day for eight months. Then, I went in that oxygen tank, followed by a radical cleanse with lymphatic drainage massages, which helped. But after years, and many surgeries and tests, I still had this chronic bone infection, called osteomyelitis, in my existing foot.

My last surgery, performed expertly by the eccentric doctor who blurted out that I looked like the mother of Norman Bates, effectively banished this infection as long as I continue to maintain a lifetime of oral antibiotics and a treatment called IVIG: a transfusion of other people's white blood cells to help bolster my immune system. This treatment is performed every six weeks in a chemo lab. I still have pain in my foot but not as horrifying as the pain when the infection becomes active.

Making it to the bathroom each morning was challenging, let alone getting myself "assembled" to feed the kids and get them to school. Sometimes, I didn't want to wake up from my dreams. In one fantasy, I was in Europe with men from my past. I was still desirable, young, and free, traveling around wherever I wanted and meeting old friends. I couldn't bear the thought of rousing from that dream. But each day I woke up with challenges I couldn't control, and the only thing I could do was control how I faced them.

Coping with prosthetics forced me to dress differently. My leg-baring tight skirts of the past, along with a menagerie of high heeled shoes and sandals, were replaced with what I called Bohemian Chic. The new styles were preferable to the edgier clothes I previously favored. They were more comfortable, forgiving, and flowing, which I came to love. Subtle can be more attractive, but I still miss my knee-grazing skirts with beautiful sandals to slide on and go.

Going from Gucci platforms to walking in a brace and prosthetic was a hard adjustment, and balancing on my right stump, which has no toes for balance, was and still is difficult. After an exhaustive search, I found the right shoemaker, and figured that if I was paying so much for an ugly shoe, I might as well buy cool designer shoes because they were cheaper and just as uncomfortable. Since my foot always hurt, I thought I might as well look good.

Being in chronic pain is exhausting. Raising children in chronic pain is an exercise in self-discipline because one must be calm, loving, a good listener, and understanding. I manage it most of the time, but too often I pass out in sheer exhaustion.

I was largely on my own with the children and spent my free moments curled up in bed, coping with pain. I tried to be brave; I tried to be strong. I stood up in the most horrible pain, but most days when nobody was around, I was in bed, begging for the needed strength to get on with my day. Thoughts of my children always motivated me; I knew it would be better for them to have their mother to guide and love them. But I also considered whether it might be better for them (and myself) if I were out of the picture, replaced by a younger and healthier version.

Thank God I decided that my children needed *me* and not a replacement.

Jim complained about the expense of my caregivers until, to keep the peace, I cut them back to under ten hours of help per week. As the medical expenses mounted, I felt increasingly guilty for disrupting our lives. I hired a housekeeper who was great at keeping house but had limited hours available, so I was still on my own with the kids in the evenings and mornings.

Sometimes, when I asked Jim to stop at the grocery store for something I forgot, he would sigh and complain that I had a whole day in which to do these things myself. I bought into this guilt. I constantly wanted to do better, to *be* better.

Jim had been so devoted to me in the hospital and had cheered me on with my initial surgery and fittings. I owed him a little normalcy, right?

I wanted to go back to the me I was before my illness, only better, sweeter, more understanding, and a great mom and a great wife. Like a horse following a carrot, and I kept after that ideal with all my strength and determination.

—w—

Money was a concern. Everything was so expensive. Not only medical care but help in the house and therapy for me and the kids was all out of pocket, so the expenses were mounting up.

I felt that Jim needed therapy as much or more than I did, but he didn't want to spend the time or the money. Even his family encouraged him to go. Jim had always been an anxious person. Even before all of this, he would suddenly and without provocation go into a full-blown panic attack. I was always there to soothe him, but now he was drinking a great deal to numb himself. His business was suffering due to the recession, and he and his business partner (who happened to be his brother) were breaking up. I listened to him and shared in his pain. Jim had gone into his own dark place, and I wanted to be there for him like he had been with me.

Jim didn't seem to ever be satisfied. Nothing was ever right or enough for him. I had married a quirky man who was shy and awkward. I had brought love, warmth, and laughter into his life, and when I needed him most, he turned on me.

Three years after my initial illness and emergency room visit, I pursued and won a medical settlement from the hospital and the emergency room doctor. I could now afford to ease Jim's financial burden; I paid off the balance of our mortgage. I used to joke with Jim that when and if I won the medical settlement, I would indulge his love for cars and buy him a Maserati. Once I won the settlement, Jim talked me into buying him the Maserati. I guess his Porsche wasn't nice enough! I hesitated but he guilted me. He said he deserved it for taking care of me. At the time, I had hoped that easing our debt load would comfort Jim and relieve his depression and anxiety, too.

Jim was a car enthusiast and always traded up cars as long as I had known him, as it was his hobby and obsession. *Newer, faster, better* was his mantra. He used to say, "Thank goodness my obsession is with cars, not girls."

My settlement needed to last me for a lifetime of medical problems, and I needed it. Jim assured me that I had more than enough, but I wasn't so sure. When the money came in, I was unsure how to protect it. I did not want to invest in the stock market and risk losing it, so I invested in conservative short-term bonds.

Jim told me he had an amazing idea. One of my closest girlfriends, Tricia, lived at the Trump Chicago with her husband, Paul, and their small daughter. We loved visiting them at the luxurious spa there. I could afford a one-bedroom apartment, which I would buy as an investment and use when I wanted to treat myself to a peaceful oasis to get some much-needed peace and quiet. I bought the condominium through my trust in my own name. Jim tried to get me to put his name on the apartment, but I would not. My attorneys advised me not to commingle my settlement money.

Almost immediately after the closing, Jim started enjoying overnights down there on his own at least once a week and sometimes twice. What began as a peaceful getaway for me turned into an escape for Jim; now I had no help at night or in the morning.

The apartment created an extra hardship because Jim had three cats who acted out in his absence by urinating on our bed. Our bedroom had the worst stench of cat urine! When I complained to Jim, he accused me of fabricating a lie to make him feel bad.

We adopted a beautiful little puppy named Marshawn, the sweetest, most adorable animal. He came to us without potty training. Marshawn needed to be walked three times a day in below-zero temperatures. I took that on myself, in the cold Chicago winter, on a post-surgical stub of a foot and a prosthetic leg, running the risk of getting gangrene.

The mornings were brutal, from getting the kids off to school and cleaning up after the cats to walking the puppy. That took so much out of me I could hardly do anything else for the rest of the day. I still had doctor's appointments and I worked part-time in the boutique until I quit that job. I started to represent and sell handbags named Hung On You, designed by Patti Hansen, the wife of Keith Richards.

I tried to accomplish a lot and make Jim and everyone else proud of me. Everyone was supportive, except for Jim, who deflated my efforts with cynicism. The house wasn't orderly enough. The boutique didn't pay enough. Nothing was ever right. But when we went out in the evening and I was dressed up and giggling with friends and Jim had loosened up with a few drinks, he would once again become the sweet, complimentary guy I had grown to love. I would reason that staying married to him was worth it.

Jim continued to stay at the apartment in the city and hang out with a new set of friends as an escape. I didn't like this new scenario too much and would say so; Jim agreed that some of his new pals were not great people, but they were good fun.

After enjoying a year or so in the city, Jim decided to buy a boat for our family to enjoy, he said. His business had enjoyed a complete resurgence and "Lucky Penny" was a beautiful boat, bigger and nicer than I thought we should get. But he was happy and excited. The boat was docked in a new harbor on the south side of Chicago and right next to us was a dear man who taught Jim about boating.

In a very short time, Jim said he needed to upgrade to a ritzier harbor where there was more action and "cooler" patrons. So off we went. Jim acted mean to me on this new boat of his, criticizing me constantly for everything, from the way I folded towels to how I dumped the garbage.

I held my ground and admonished him for his bully-ing. He would never apologize but explained that he was nervous about being a captain. After Jim traded in the Maserati for a series of four different cars, including a Tesla and a Corvette, he decided that his new boat wasn't good enough either, so he traded it in for one double in size. He said it would be more comfortable than his first boat, which had too many mechanical problems.

Instead of *Lucky Penny Two,* he named his new boat *Game Changer.* Can you guess what happened next?

Chapter Eleven:
Divorce

"I know not what the future holds, but I know who holds the future." —Homer

I finally regained a substantial amount of physical and psychological control over my daily life, and slowly but surely, I put these carefully developed and finely tuned changes into action, opening surprising new doors and opportunities.

The biggest part of my journey continued on a spiritual front. As I triumphed through a series of miraculous physical recoveries, I found unexpected strength in what I couldn't see—internal forces guiding me and providing staples of faith—to survive and thrive. I went from being a woman confident in her beauty to one forced to face an endless string of humiliations. I could no longer control my body, let alone how others perceived me.

I could not take anything for granted. This meant a serious re-evaluation of my priorities, from how I valued myself to my friends and colleagues, and most important, how this affected my marriage and my role as a mother to two adolescent children.

I learned how humor, grace, and love can determine how we handle adversity. I relied on those qualities when my marriage did not survive. While I tried to construct a new life for myself, our two kids were in desperate need of at least one stable parent.

Men tend to shut down when they want out; they don't know how to communicate this. Instead, they check out completely, leaving their partners without badly needed closure.

After so much turmoil and hard-won physical recoveries, I still had a battle to fight in divorce court. Our divorce was an unexpected hurdle coming after all the intense challenges I faced. I held on to anything positive in those early months. One of my coping mechanisms was to remind myself of what I had rather than focusing on what I had lost.

Of course, divorce is tragic for everyone involved, and mine was long and difficult, the process painstakingly played out in court for years, where I struggled to be seen and heard, let alone respected. Luckily, the judge took my side, and for the first time in her thirty years on the bench, she was brought to tears. I felt protected in her courtroom, just as I had felt secure with the mediator who ultimately won my settlement against the hospital. I welcomed a new beginning and I eventually found greater joy in living for myself and my children than bending myself in every direction to please someone who was never happy.

On top of the maladies I dealt with all day long, I had to comfort and console two heart-broken children. I tried to put on a brave and cheerful front for Sloane and Ross, but I was scared and angry and in constant pain. It was hard to pretend I was okay.

Many women at fifty feel changes in their bodies. I was facing fifty with a body that felt embarrassing and humiliating. It wasn't just a leg; it was all my extremities. It would be daunting to reveal one's body and soul to someone new after being married for seventeen years. I was now middle aged and handicapped, but I was convinced that a love life should still be possible for me. After all, my long marriage was so unsatisfying in every way—sexually, emotionally, and spiritually.

When I was young, I was bad at choosing relationships. I seemed to choose the safe bet but then I would grow disappointed and critical of my partner. I couldn't seem to get it right. For some reason, I didn't truly enjoy the men I met but I took what was offered. That is how I met and married Jim, in a haze of indifference. I was tired of waiting for what I had not experienced yet in love, so I entered my marriage apprehensive but resigned.

One late summer evening before our divorce, Jim and I had our babysitter come early. We had plans to go out for dinner after a session with our family counselor, Geri, a disarming and comforting lady, who had a warm elegance about her. As we sat down on her cozy chairs, I was flush with excitement. With Jim and me going to work on our sixteen-year marriage, I felt the worst was over for our family. We had gotten through most of the stages of our recovery and grief and were finally enjoying some financial freedom after a rough period.

Just as I began to share these positive feelings, Jim spoke over me, as he so often did. "I'm not attracted to Penny anymore." His flat announcement came without warning. "I have a lot of younger girls that come on my boat and one of them called me sexy."

Jim was bragging to Geri, the last thing I expected to hear. When asked to elaborate, he blushed and sputtered about the new life he had been living secretly but not too carefully right under my nose! Up until then, I had been unbelievably trusting and naïve.

For months, I had asked Jim why my personal items were missing from his boat. I kept a suitcase there, full of beautiful clothes, jewelry, and makeup, but Jim claimed it was just me being careless and forgetful like always.

I believe the word for this is *gaslighting*.

Yes, I was being gaslit, right there in Geri's office, like an unsuspecting, clueless wife in an Alfred Hitchcock film. I felt as if I had just been slapped, hard. Then Jim admitted that he struggled sexually since my "accident" and felt he was too young to be sexually inactive. He saw me as damaged goods.

Driving around in his new Maserati, bought with my blood money, and sporting a new boat that he bought with his own nouveau riche wealth, Jim presented himself around town as a rich man. None of his young boat girls knew he had a severely sick wife caring for their kids in a big house in the suburbs.

I was floored by his admission in our therapy session, and I walked out of that appointment in a haze. Jim acted as if it was business as usual. He went off to relax on his boat instead of coming home with me, which, for the first time ever, I begged him to do so we could work together to save what was left, to keep our family together.

A flurry of images and memories overwhelmed me.

When he came home after buying his second boat, *The Game Changer,* he was so proud of his purchase. I hugged him and asked if we could go to dinner the next night, just the two of us. Jim refused, telling me he was going to a party and that I wasn't invited. I pleaded with him to stay home with me, that our marriage was in crisis. I was a wreck and needed to be with him.

I should have known right then. Jim's lack of integrity or conscience never ceased to amaze and disappoint me. Unfortunately, men do leave their families, but in my situation, the divisive way he handled things was an anomaly, even to the most jaded attorneys.

Jim's personal agenda trumped everything. If I called him with a question about our house, he refused to answer. If I begged him to drive the kids in a carpool, he refused, chiding me that I didn't give him ample warning. He was a busy man, after all, and how could I not remember that?

Sometimes, when we cannot change things, when we are forced to adapt, we discover something deep inside us that enables us to prevail and prosper. The man I had devoted myself to for seventeen years had become an alien to me and if I had to amputate a few body parts to be rightfully rid of him, so be it. In some weird way, it was almost worth the price I had to pay.

—⚍—

When Jim finally left, I knew that it meant the end of our relationship and I acted accordingly, serving him with divorce papers and making him move out of our family home. I had been accommodating to a fault for so long, thinking he was aware and cognizant of all my concessions and sacrifices. I treated him well despite everything. The decision was easy and right for me. However, my children did not fully understand, and it was hard to remain on the high road. I kept my mouth shut as much as I could, while Jim told them I had kicked him out for no good reason. I was in the untenable position of caring for my children's broken hearts while he disappeared. I never had a moment to vent because Sloan and Ross were always glued to me, and I tried not to talk about their dad around them. I tried to explain his crazy behavior when I couldn't wrap my head around it myself. They were still small and didn't understand why or what was happening, and I needed to keep my lip zipped and focus on them, but inside I was appalled.

Making that situation right with Ross and Sloan became my primary goal, and I put my attention on our new path forward.

Sometimes we walk to the altar unsure of our life ahead. I felt a bit boxed into my decision to get married, but once I made the commitment, I was all in and hoped for the best. I loved being a mother for the first time, at thirty-nine years old, and devoted myself to my family life even though my heart was heavy because I had lost my mother midway through my first pregnancy. This left a giant void as I wanted to enjoy my adorable babies with her. It was tragic but I kept soldiering on as new moms do.

When my Sloan was born, I had another devastating blow when my Aunt Myrna passed away the same day. I convinced myself of the circle of life, but I was grieving over both these losses while I became a mother.

The people we marry sometimes turn out to be much different than what we imagine. In my case, Jim seemed to morph from who I thought he was, the sweetest most devoted man, into essentially neither of those things. Sixteen years later, Jim greatly disrespected me and our marriage in much the way that my first husband did many years before.

I would never have compared the two men but as time went on Jim displayed a similar out-of-control behavior that Stan did. Two different men making promises that they never intended to keep. I examined my own behavior and knew that I did not deserve any of that.

So, what made Jim, a seemingly angelic boy, spin himself into a self-serving, egotistical lout? I suppose I was different than a lot of other women, in that I would deny myself and play it safe, afraid of getting hurt and even worse, terrified of hurting someone else. I sacrificed my own happiness to give someone else theirs. This has been a pattern all my life.

I thought I had to be the bravest person ever to get through the physical challenges I endured, but divorcing my husband was even harder. I know people face hard things all the time, but it took everything I had to get through it.

To anyone who knows the world of divorce, they know that becoming an independent woman of strength and integrity requires bravery, balls, and a bit of luck. In my case, which I doubt is unique, it was a question of ensuring my comfort and long-term survival. I had to do it— for myself and my kids.

When I met Jim, he was tall, handsome, and success-ful. But he changed in many respects. The person I used to love who looked after me so gently through my ordeal faded to a ghost of his former self, a distant relic of our past. He seemed wonderful during my initial recovery and took me on a romantic cruise three months after I learned to walk again. But six years later, it simply wasn't the same.

He'd lost interest in being friends or lovers. His trans-formation was disturbing and confusing. By the time

I finally realized the enormity of the change, my close friends and family had already come to their conclusions and were angry at Jim and concerned about me.

"Penny, what are you waiting for?"

In the end, I had no choice because I knew it was the best choice for everyone, despite the upheaval divorce caused our children. Sloan had a tough time and became confused and sad for a while before turning those feelings harshly at me or anyone else in her path. Ross dealt in his own way, keeping his feelings inside.

I survived the humiliation of a failed marriage because I knew who I was, no matter how much I suffered and struggled with the daily challenges of my body. Taking control of my life has been liberating. It was the right thing to do. In the end, I felt reborn, happy that I took the necessary steps to move on with my life as a single woman and mother.

Chapter Twelve:
Renewal

"Even his griefs are a joy long after to one that remembers
all that he wrought and endured." —Homer

Through shock and aftershock, my tale of survival and
renewal goes far beyond the physical, emotional, and
psychological realms one might expect. Over the past ten
years, it has become the odyssey of my soul.

Overcoming severe trauma required reconstructing
who I am, piece by piece, so that I could regain self-
respect and self-esteem under the toughest conditions
imaginable. My attitude has invited new love into my
life and has made adjusting to an empty nest much easier.
My children and I became survivors of a shipwreck and
clung to each other through dark times. We are closer
now than ever as they venture into a world of their own,
secure in their ability to adapt and cope with uncertainty
and the unexpected.

I was taught at an early age that I wouldn't be as lovable
if I spoke my mind or created waves. I came to be well-
liked, but at my own expense. In a moment of reckoning,

in the emergency room that fateful day of November 28, 2008, drowning my inner voice nearly killed me. That silent scream manufactured a million future cries.

When I heard a voice telling me to remember my own power, I knew it was a forewarning of odious consequences. When I heard *that* voice, I knew it was God. It was real. I knew I was in trouble.

I remember the first time I began to disengage from my inner voice. It was when I was about twelve and our family had adopted a kitten named Fluff. My older brother Scott used to get up early so he could be the first one to free our cat from the laundry room.

One morning, I got downstairs first to hold Fluff's warm, furry body when suddenly I felt my head explode! Scott had smashed my face into the hard cement pavement. He scooped up our kitty without any concern or backward glance to ask if I was okay. I was hurt, angry, and humiliated. I developed a black eye and a fat lip. I was not only in a lot of pain, but my brother's insolence greatly troubled me.

Even more upsetting was my mother's lack of concern for my welfare. As I shouted at my parents, they victim-shamed me. In front of Scott, they blamed me for how I reacted: my shouting canceled out his physical attack. They made me feel that my explosive behavior was worse than his.

This experience profoundly affected me. From that day forward, I felt ashamed to express myself in any negative way. I saw my mother as the ultimate judge, and her judgement made me feel I needed to be agreeable no matter what, even if it meant silencing my own voice. The lesson continued as I matured, that I must never speak out in confrontation to others.

I became the most laid back, non-confrontational version of myself I could manage, but the strain of not allowing myself meaningful expression caused me to doubt my own voice.

That left me ripe for the disaster that befell me in November. I knew I needed a second opinion after initial evaluation. I vividly remember requesting a deeper dive into my symptoms, but I was not heard. As so often happened in my marriage, as well as throughout my childhood, I was silenced.

God marked that emergency room incident for me in a dramatic way, not to scold but to teach me the importance of speaking up for myself, to express my opinions without fear.

Through the years, I adapted a persona of an easy going and happy-go-lucky girl. Although attractive on a surface level, this attitude did not serve me well personally. The day I was wheeled into that emergency room I was ashamed to argue or speak out; I wanted that handsome emergency room doctor to find me agreeable.

I lay there in the worst possible physical distress, trying to be liked by someone I didn't know, keeping my mouth shut at my own peril. I almost died for fear of someone thinking I was obnoxious. The consequences of my silence are still unraveling and will be a permanent regret, one I can never forget.

Through revisiting my first traumatic experience, the one that caused me to stunt my authentic voice for a very long time, I hope that I can convey the importance of honoring yourself. We have a voice for a reason.

—∞—

I grew up feeling beautiful. I'm sure I wasn't as beautiful as I felt, but a healthy dose of self-confidence, obvious joy, and an easy laugh (mixed with personal style) can be attractive. These qualities make a mildly attractive woman into a more desirable one. For most of my teens and adulthood, I enjoyed the perks of being a somewhat alluring woman.

What happens then, when that same woman becomes deathly ill, unable to advocate for herself in a life and death situation, where even her medical evaluation and treatment is based almost solely on her appearance? What happens when that woman, who felt relatively invincible, gets literally and irreparably torn apart, physically and emotionally?

What then becomes the opposite of beauty?

If she is strong, determined, and owns her inner beauty, she can channel that through the worst nightmare imaginable. In a short period of time, I went from pretty and alluring to unsightly. I went from turning heads to people turning away, unable to look at me.

When I was stuck in my wheelchair, I looked straight at people, willing them to see the real me. I wanted them to see beyond the wheelchair to the beauty I still had inside.

After an arduous uphill battle to reclaim my health, including the ability to stand up and walk away from that wheelchair, I needed to make tough decisions that would ultimately lead me to discover my own new happiness.

Five years after nearly dying, I filed for divorce. It required courage to live on my own as a single mother with my handicaps. I can't say I recommend it, but I guess I do.

One year after our separation, I felt reborn. Now, I am my best self, and genuinely happy I took the risk. I have redefined what is beautiful. What I first thought was ugly is exactly what made me strong enough to reinvent myself. Throughout my struggle, I found trust and faith and a healthy dose of self-love. What could be more beautiful than that?

When a woman marries, has children, and passes fifty, she might think her best days are over. Not me. I do not focus on my limitations, of which there are plenty. When I feel the urge to hide something, I dress up in a sexy outfit with an open back. I have always been courageous, optimistic, and motivated, but now that these attributes have been tested to the max, I appreciate them even more.

Each day when I wake up, I wonder how I will get through the day. I put on my left liner, sock, and prosthetic, put my right foot in a protective bandage with a special sock, a foot brace and shoe filler, followed by my actual shoe. I go to the bathroom and take my requisite meds. I am usually knocked out by then and feeling tired, ill, and in pain. I sit down in a chairlift and ride down my home staircase. I feed the dog and take him for a walk—with a smile on my face. By the time these "normal" activities are done, I usually lie down and pray to feel better—if not for me then for my beloved children and family—and then for me because I deserve it. We all do!

Inside, I might be writhing in pain under my beautiful clothes. My body, which I kept slim and toned through healthy eating and consistent exercise, has been irreversibly altered from the neck down. There is not one area, from my tracheal scar at my throat to my missing toes, which has not been altered surgically as a result of this heinous event, called toxic shock syndrome. It was the catalyst for all the other problems I currently suffer with and will face forever.

On the outside, I am a smiling, fit woman. Inside, I am a new rendition of the tin man. Each day is a monumental struggle, but thankfully I have two wonderful children to distract me from the pain and keep me focused on bigger and better things.

When my head and heart are in the right place, and family and friends are at my side, I feel like I can do anything. Any woman grappling with challenges *can* draw on her personal strength because each of us have a bigger reservoir than we imagine. Trust yourself, love yourself, and honor your inner voice.

Chapter Thirteen:
Adaptive Adventures

"The charity that is a trifle to us can be precious to others."
—Homer

I eventually became an avid skier, biker, dancer, and tennis player. I have put that new knowledge to good use through my work with Adaptive Adventures (AA), a non-profit dedicated to helping people with physical disabilities become proficient in a variety of outdoor sports. For each newly challenged person I meet, I am living proof of these possibilities.

AA was co-founded by Matt Feeney and Joel Berman. Both men suffer from disabilities. Joel is an above knee amputee and Matt is partially paralyzed from a diving accident. These men are amazing and serve as inspirational figures in the disability world.

I met many others in AA who helped me keep my own situation in perspective. Becoming an activist for disabled people has been so rewarding. I offer advice, support, and empathy as only someone who has experienced such an ordeal can do. I've found that healing others is the best way to heal yourself. If you engage with people, you learn a lot. It's like having a front row seat to the movie called life.

For example, Sergeant Brad Shwarz gave me a sense of the emotional damage of serving in a war. I sat next to him on a flight we were both taking to Steamboat Springs, Colorado, on our way to a ski camp hosted by AA. Brad had entered the army at nineteen. As a toddler, he played with his GI Joes, and all he ever wanted was to be a soldier. At twenty he was deployed to Iraq. Brad became a marksman who could shoot a moving target with great accuracy. At age twenty-one, he led his team into battles, protecting our country from terrorism and weapons of mass destruction.

Brad came back from his second deployment some-what whole but not well. He was hit by a roadside bomb and suffered traumatic brain injury, TBI, and back, spine, and leg damage. He also lost several of his soldier brothers in that ambush. After being hit by the roadside bomb, he was airlifted back home to the safety of the VA hospital in Georgia.

My injuries are different than his; mine are external, Brad's are mostly internal. Interestingly, although I am missing limbs, I look less injured than Brad. In our several hours together flying and driving to our destination, I got a sense of the emotional damage war has wrought on this young man.

Before boarding our flight, Brad approached the gate limping on a cane. He speaks with slight difficulty and suffers from both thirty-seven percent short term memory loss and twenty percent long term loss. He is a dead ringer for Joaquin Phoenix. He is bright, witty, honest, and deep, and in this short time, we bonded and shared our life histories. I respect and admire this young soul who has been rehabilitated through the efforts of Adaptive Adventures, as it would be a tragedy to lose this man through his pain. Brad told me that he has a five-year-old daughter that he lives for and cares for; she and his guide dog saved him.

At twenty-nine, Brad is on permanent disability. During his first six years home, he struggled with suicidal urges; his girlfriend left him and took their four-month-old child away, and he missed his army buddies who were a part of him. He also missed being in the war zone, where he felt like his true self, doing what he was good at, what he was born to do.

The terrible truth is that once soldiers like Brad are home from their detail, they feel misplaced in civilian life. Brad and other young soldiers are trained to lead and protect and are often addicted to the action and the adrenaline rush of combat. Back at home, Brad could only find work as an administration assistant at Sears Roebuck. He struggled with drug and alcohol addiction as well as anger management, all related to post-traumatic stress disorder, or PTSD.

There are many thousands of people walking around with PTSD. The sad news is that PTSD affects not only these young soldiers but also their families, passing trauma in one form or another down through generations.

Brad found Adaptive Adventures and joined the dragon race paddle boat team. He became involved and engaged through active sports. Through extreme sports, veterans can feel that adrenaline rush or "high" in a healthy way and also bond with people who have similar experiences. Many of these men who openly shared their lives with me were happy and engaged; some, if not all, of them had been on the brink of quitting living before finding this new world of hope and togetherness.

In the autumn, Adaptive Adventures stages its Challenge Tour to raise money. I love riding my bike in this event and getting friends to join. I met an inspirational young man named Aaron who had an ATV accident and is now living in a wheelchair. If we can give him a half hour of riding an adaptive hand cycle that comes through our donations, there is no greater gift. It's people like Aaron that spur me on to do these fundraising events so he can enjoy a rewarding life. Charity is fulfilling, and by helping others you can really help yourself.

Chapter Fourteen: Gratitude

"We must set aside old notions and embrace fresh ones; and, as we learn, we must be daily unlearning something which it has cost us no small labour and anxiety to acquire." —Homer

People often ask me, "How do you do it?" That question is hard to answer. It's taken a lot of time, but I think it comes down to self-worth. It's about me knowing and saying that I'm worth it. I have to keep pushing through until I can't anymore. I have to make it better. I *will* make it better.

I remember being told that I will find my way back to myself, my fashionable self. There were times when I looked in the mirror and couldn't imagine it happening. But somewhere deep down, I believed I would climb slowly back. And I have. Yet I know that many people can't do so.

It is a full-circle moment for me now. I'm out. I'm laughing. I'm feeling fashionable and beautiful again. I love and am loved. I treasure every moment and encourage others to never give up on themselves or their dreams.

Many who knew me had faith that I could pull through what seemed like an impossible ordeal but were still surprised to see how I got myself put back together, piece by piece, where I now look much the same as before. People often forget what happened. But it is impossible for me to ever forget.

Anyone who has survived a life-threatening trauma knows how it makes one aware of things we take for granted: seeing, sitting, eating, drinking, talking, walking, even using one's own hands. Since I had to work so hard to regain any semblance of these capabilities, I have come to appreciate even the smallest freedoms these physical activities represent. My capacity to appreciate the simple things in life has never waned. Now, each and every day, I take nothing for granted.

My medical history has been well documented. My recovery defies explanation. The cause of this tragic illness has never been explained by a medical team of experts. I have become a different person—physically and spiritually—as a result of this experience.

In 2008, I was enjoying an indulgent life of health, freedom, and privilege, oblivious to the world around me and out of touch with what didn't concern me. For reasons unknown to me at the time, I felt dissatisfied, disingenuous, and not fully present.

When I became sick, any internal journey detoured into a solitary stroll through the valley of death. I was stuck behind a curtain of unconsciousness, and even after waking, I did not realize I stood at the crossroads of life and death.

Death presented itself as the more lovely choice, like a dream sequence experienced in an alternate life. I envisioned myself gently walking on a path toward a country garden, floating ecstatically over a simple white fence, hearing my favorite Beatles song become louder and clearer as I approached a gate.

I felt I was not asleep but experiencing something surreal in another place and time. No matter how I tried, I could not duplicate that feeling. Once I awoke, I couldn't find that chapter, and Jackie could not recall reading it. Several of my friends apparently read to me from the Lennon book at my bedside but nobody recalls that specific part. During my first year out of coma I constantly searched for this paragraph, the one that had given me such a deep feeling of pleasure, but I never found it.

During my seventy-six days suspended in a coma, I was swept up in a vortex of something inexplicable. Since that vision, I do not fear death. I hope my tale will offer solace to those grieving the loss of a loved one. Death is harder for those left behind, since the one passing goes to a place of peace.

Before any of this happened, I used to toy with the notion that our lives were perhaps predetermined and played out like a theater play. My experience has changed those beliefs. Now, I believe our action or inaction is the driving force that maps out our personal destinies. Yes, we are born to certain unique and personal environmental and physical characteristics, but we are ultimately the directors of our own movies with many surprising plot twists.

My story may seem momentous because few people come back from such a traumatic event after seeing a glimpse of the world beyond. While I do not claim to know any secrets of mankind, I believe there is profound meaning in our existence.

This book has been written with the best of intentions. By sharing my pivotal experiences with near death and living through an altered state, I am not seeking pity or praise. Instead, I want to remind people of the transformative nature of life and how trauma and catastrophe can trigger enormous positive change. Through my experiences I have come to feel closer to the presence of a divine nature, which has allowed me to see things about life and people with more depth and clarity.

This psychological and spiritual change in me is for the better, especially when it comes to the physical pain and challenges I still must endure. I hope and pray this brings comfort for those contemplating what happens when we die. Yes, we will go someplace glorious when the time is right. For now, I am determined to enjoy this splendor on Earth.

Epilogue

"Any moment might be our last. Everything is more beautiful because we're doomed. You will never be lovelier than you are now. We will never be here again" —Homer, *The Iliad*

I named my book *Aftershock* because the initial toxic shock was only the beginning. My quest to regain my life and my recovery was like a virtual minefield of problems and various unknowns.

My metaphorical rebirth has had a profound effect on me, both positively and negatively. Spiritually, I grew exponentially but my physical collateral damage reminds me all too often of my crash. If not for my injuries I might not reflect on my ordeal as often as I do now.

My physical collapse diverted my life direction and pushed me to evolve in ways that were important and defining. I am living a more authentic life now and calling my own shots. It was scary at first to live on my own and make the big decisions all alone, but now I wouldn't change it because I grew in so many different ways. Mostly being the head of my own household and raising my children as I saw fit. Those initial years were more difficult than I can describe, but I feel as though I made it through many difficult tests. If I could go back and change anything it would be to reverse the collateral damage that my family and I endured.

Not many people get to attend their own funerals. I feel as if I did because I was able to read and hear condolences of love and admiration from most everyone that I had ever known and even from some folks that I was only acquainted with. After I awoke and was lucid enough and had some restored eyesight I was given a big crocodile skin box filled with love letters written by family, friends and people from my community. I felt incredibly validated when I learned how people had seen me for who I was; they commented on how warm, friendly, and open I was. I never realized how loved and appreciated I was and that feeling still fortifies me and helps me get through the tough times. The love and care I received throughout my ordeal pushed me to go on.

It's interesting that I should have more confidence ;now than ever before. Knowing how valued I am, how loved is more gratifying to me than having a perfect body.

Love came through my coma dreams and when I recognized my visitors. They were the constant and daily people who never left me alone even when I was asleep. Often my visitors showed up for a short while to protect me or enquire about my health. Oftentimes my mother-in-law would ride up to me on a white stallion checking to see if I was still hanging in there and happily rode away when I assured her that I still was.

There is no doubt in my mind that comatose people can hear us.

Sometimes my visions were terrible and dark, but then they would ultimately blossom into a golden, light-filled fantasy where I felt buoyant and wonderfully care-free. There was a feeling for a quick second of a profound ecstasy that I will never forget. I badly wanted to stay in that moment forever. I tried to conjure that mystical feeling again and I could not.

I believe that I was at the crossroads between life and death in that nanosecond of time. I was turned back from the precipice to tell this wondrous story and share my love of life and humanity.

If Life is a play or a book, then this is my personal story.

I feel comfort knowing I will feel this bliss again when it is my final time. For now, I will try to impart comfort in knowing that we experience glory in the end.

That is my belief.

That was my experience.

Could it be possible that we experience complete bliss or a rapture towards the end of our lives as an ultimate reward for life and its tough challenges?

Since then, I have read others' accounts of near death experiences (NDE). Like myself, other survivors report similar dreams that were dark, like being underground or in a cave. Many describe visions of rats and frightening animals, eventually giving way to a sort of musical the-atre and a connection to the universe. I felt a weightless feeling and a lack of worry or fear. Like joy overcame every part of me.

I remember being at one with the heavenly music and feeling a happiness so profound it was almost unrecognizable. The culmination of that split second changed me forever. I feel fortunate to have experienced it.

I entered into another dimension. While some skeptics may try to explain that it was my brains' reaction to a chemical output and the possible release of pure dopamine when we are about to die, I still feel a gratitude for what I call my incredible baptism.

For me it was a metaphor for life—lightness and darkness; darkness and light.

Twice I have whispered into the ear of loved ones hanging on to the last breath of their lives—I wanted them to know that once they let go, there was nothing to fear. I prayed for them to find their peace and bliss. Judging from their final expressions, they both seemed to have found it.

Years prior, I was pleasantly surprised to see a beatific smile on own my mothers face as she lay in a hospital bed striped with the freezing winter sun alighting her beautiful features. I had witnessed her fear of her cancer as she went from doctor to doctor. She hoped to hear a better verdict on her health but unfortunately she died within a year of her initial diagnosis. I felt some small measure of solace seeing her look relieved of her constant pain and anxiety, but the world felt so much lonelier when she was gone.

Almost ten years later, after my own experience with near death, I began to see the world in multicolor again, as if I had come back to my younger self with hopes and dreams of a better and more recognizable life.

After the initial shock and insult wore off, I began to feel liberated and excited. I now try to live a joyous, uncensored,free life full of music, dancing, learning, laughing and connecting.

Currently my days are like waves. Some days are higher than others. Most days begin with a sort of dread but usually end on a good note with gratitude and fulfillment in my heart. Gratitude because I have traveled to places with people on various missions of charity that I would never have experienced before. I explored Ecuador with Range of Motion Project (Romp), a high point where I enjoyed climbing and hiking and exploring other cultures. I went with the same group to Honduras and enjoyed helping other people get through similar afflictions that I had survived. Earlier I mentioned another charity I love called Adaptive Adventures which taught me how to ski again and bike distances. I camped with both organizations and am so happy that I did. All of it helped me gain important perspective and helped me feel less alone in my plight.

Presently I am somewhat content but many times I feel tired just thinking about what I have to do to get myself up for a cup of coffee. I awaken and turn over to see my heavy prosthetic leg sitting next to my bed and I already feel exhausted. Putting on my leg is a two-step process. So is my shoe liner and my digits on both hands, never mind contact lenses and our other regular endeavors. I typically pull myself together with an attractive outfit for the day because the cuter the outfit, the better I feel.

I then go face the world which more often than not smiles back on me.

I am such a social person that most human contact fuels me to thrive. I find ways to connect with almost anyone that I meet. This has been my greatest gift, one I honed in on in the years since what feels like my death and my resurrection.

I am fulfilled by sharing my life with all of you through this book. It has been meaningful and cathartic to write.

Thank you for caring.

For more short stories on my coma dreams and visions please check out my blog and website at pennyfisher1.

Acknowledgements

To start I must mention that my friends have been my life support for without them I would not have lived.

My oldest and dearest best friends Laura, Alissa, Christina, and Deanne are my core. The four of us have an intimacy and a history that goes far back, more than thirty years. Having lost my parents at a fairly young age, these three ladies jumped in and have been my chosen family ever since. Laura and Alissa especially are very close to my children, never forgetting their birthdays and spoiling and loving them like true Aunties.

Jackie and Danielle, my suburban neighbors, and very close "newer" friends of the last twenty-two years. Jackie was the first person to arrive at my hospital bed and the last person I called to tell her that I knew I was dying. Jackie flew across the country within twenty-four hours of hearing I was in coma. When she got there at midnight, a nurse asked her to find Jim and tell him to come back because I wasn't going to make it through the hour. Jackie tracked him down and while he was on his way back, she went into my dark scary room with the sound of the life force machines. She picked up the book of John Lennon which I carried everywhere and began to read to me.

Just then, my vitals began to recover. Jackie's voice broke the surface, and I had the near death experience listening to her beautifully melodic voice. The staff was honestly floored that I rallied. Jackie saved my life. People need people, especially warm loving people like my best friends of which there are many. Lucky me.

When I was finally home from all the hospitals that every one of my close friends came and traveled to, I was trying to reintegrate into my normal life. I felt so alone and vulnerable in my big house with no mobility. Every single day I would hear the rumble of my garage door opening, and I would see either Jackie or Danielle's lovely faces as one or the other peeked into my bedroom, ready to bathe me, drive me or any other task at hand. They took turns, putting their own lives on hold as I tried to rehabilitate

Pam Fisher, my sister-in-law, gave up many months of her own life to manage my complete care. I became so dependent on her strength and her logic that it was difficult to detach. I couldn't go a day without seeing her. She was my Rock.

My other sister-in-law, Michele, came almost every day and put hair and make up on me to present me to my children when they were coming to see me. Her words of encouragement were beautiful and sincere. My father-in-law and mother-in-law were also there constantly with love and care.

Dr. William Pearce, my main surgeon, who became a friend to me, lending hope and normalcy and a few giggles to the darkest chapter of my life. All the nurses who cared for me in those early days. Dr. Lu, a plastic surgeon who offered to help out of the goodness of his heart, did my complete wound care for free when I could no longer visit my hospital doctors in the hospital after I was home.

Cousins Danielle and Stephanie, who came and sat in the first hospital for days waiting for news. Stu and Kylene, my other cousins, who came to see me twice, once in hospital and once in Chicago. Kylene pilots her own small plane and flew my brother in to see me while I was still in coma. Some of those stories of them flying together is a comedy in itself.

My brother, Scott was terrific in hospital, very smart and scientific. He was calm and gave prudent advice. He called me each and every day and still does. Jeanette and Rachel. who came over every day when I was back home as did cousins Pam and Adrienne. Love you all.

Josie, another friend who came over with her husband to do hair, makeup, facials, and anything else. Andi, who took me out every Thursday on some magical excursions that I always looked forward to. Andi, Josie, and Josie's husband Anthony, I will always appreciate your loving kindness and care.

Cindy Smith, a local spin teacher who weight trained me in those early months along with Stephanie Adler who came over to teach me yoga. Both ladies offered their time and expertise free of charge, as did my BFFL

Randi, who made my core strong with private Pilates lessons so I could walk again. Randi came over as often as she could while she was going through her own life transition and gave me love and support in every way, and still does. She is part of My original lake girls who I thank for making my life exciting and fun again.

Honestly, there are too many people that I love and adore and can't thank enough. I hope you know who you are.

Jill, Cheryl, Tricia. Love you all.

It takes a village, and I had one.

About the Author

Penny Fisher not only survived an unthinkable trauma, she has thrived. Raising two young kids alone in a big house without family or neighbors, just the help of her devoted and miraculous friends as she managed to raise two amazing and successful young adults. No easy feat in any condition much less sick and solo. Penny lives in her native hometown of Chicago and writes, reads, and speaks at public forums.